Christology

Christology

How Do We Talk about Jesus Christ Today?

Ralf K. Wüstenberg

Translation by Martin Rumscheidt in association with
Christine Schliesser and Randi H. Lundell

CASCADE *Books* • Eugene, Oregon

CHRISTOLOGY
How Do We Talk about Jesus Christ Today?

Copyright © 2014 Ralf K. Wüstenberg. All rights reserved. Except for brief quotations in critical publications or reviews, no part of this book may be reproduced in any manner without prior written permission from the publisher. Write: Permissions, Wipf and Stock Publishers, 199 W. 8th Ave., Suite 3, Eugene, OR 97401.

Original German-language edition, *Christologie* by Ralf K. Wüstenberg, published by Guterslöher Verlagshaus, 2009. English-language edition printed by permission.

Cascade Books
An Imprint of Wipf and Stock Publishers
199 W. 8th Ave., Suite 3
Eugene, OR 97401

www.wipfandstock.com

ISBN 13: 978-1-61097-170-6

Cataloging-in-Publication data:

Wüstenberg, Ralf K., 1965–

    Christology : how do we talk about Jesus Christ today? / Ralf K. Wüstenberg ; translation by Martin Rumscheidt in association with Christine Schliesser and Randi H. Lundell.

    x + 130 p.; 22 cm. —Includes bibliographical references.

    ISBN 13: 978-1-61097-170-6

    1. Jesus Christ—Person and offices. I. Rumscheidt, Martin. II. Schliesser, Christine, 1977–. III. Lundell, Randi H. IV. Title.

BT202 .W87 2014

Manufactured in the USA

To my mother Erika

Contents

Preface ix

1 Is a Christology at all Possible? 1
2 Accepting the Challenges 7
3 Christology in a World of Progress and Historical Scholarship 22
4 Christology in a World of Spiritual Searching 40
5 Christology in a World of Humanism and Human Rights 65
6 Christology in a World of Gender Equality 88
7 Speaking of Christ Today—Some Room for Encouragement 116

Bibliography 121

Preface

The much-heralded resurgence of religion does not necessarily mean a return to the Christian proclamation of God. In today's world, whoever speaks in a naïve way about Jesus Christ is immediately confronted by arguments. Doesn't faith in Jesus Christ necessarily also make one intolerant? How can a loving God condone the death of his Son? Isn't the whole thing about Jesus just some kind of fantasy?

This book seeks to present a clear, concise and coherent introduction into christological thought and furthermore to empower a confident discussion of Christology for today. Whoever seeks to engage in discourse on the meaning of Christian faith in society and to help shape that discourse requires theological knowledge and, more importantly, a christological foundation.

This book would therefore not have been possible without the aid of those intensively engaged listeners who attended my theological lectures at Freie Universität Berlin, Universität Flensburg and Cambridge University (UK). I am particularly indebted to my colleague, Professor Christiane Tietz, University of Zürich who read carefully and discussed critically the manuscript with me. I am also indebted to Mr. René Koch. As a former graduate of the High School for the Arts in Dresden, he provided the graphics and drawings that have inspired many discussions and have found their way into this volume, although in limited number. I am deeply indebted to Professor Martin Rumscheidt who together with Dr. Christine Schliesser and Ms. Randi Lundell provided this fine translation.

The book is dedicated to my mother, Erika Wüstenberg.

Ralf Karolus Wüstenberg
Berlin, January 2014

1

Is a Christology at all Possible?

The Case for Uncertainty

At rollicking celebrations during my student days in Berlin and Heidelberg, I was asked a question I did not like: "What are you studying?" After responding candidly, "Protestant theology," the cheerful and carefree party atmosphere regularly turned into a brooding and gloomy discussion. Great, here was the God question, and the Christian one at that! How I would have liked to deny that I was studying theology and say instead "physics" or "medicine"—or any other secular subject. Or, if I did study religion, why couldn't it be religious *studies*, something more obviously scholarly and objective? The topic of Christian theology always provoked the volunteering of further information, even when I was not in the mood after a long day of studying. "Why theology?" was the most common question asked, at least by those who had friendly intentions. The famous "why" question, I quickly learned, serves the purpose of categorizing what is presumably foreign and potentially exotic among what we know in the world. The Christian discussion about God does not belong in our world anymore; what it talks about is certainly not as self-evident as the subject matter of other disciplines. Why is this? My first response is:

- Connecting Christian theology to what is Christian—that is, connecting religious truth to one particular person—clearly goes against the *zeitgeist*. Where earlier there was a basic religious consciousness, today an exclusive connection of such a consciousness to the person of Jesus is perceived as strange or, at the very least, narrow-minded. Is Christology thus limited with respect to dialogue—within its own culture, with other religions, or with the Jews?

- The general interest in religious questions that we observe today does not correspond to an interest in developing a systematic doctrine about Jesus Christ. Interestingly enough, it appears that the rediscovery of Jesus in Europe (in literature, in philosophy, and in other religions)[1] has not meant the reflection on his specific relationship to God. Has Christology served its time as a "cold dogmatic faith"? Is not the word *Christology* itself perhaps an inappropriate objectification of the living God, making it all too "academic"?[2]

- The period of religious theories and of their systematic development, which would also assign Christology a place, is apparently over. Does Dietrich Bonhoeffer's prognosis of the emergence of religionlessness[3] apply in particular to Christology, since in the midst of irreversible secularization and religious plurality he had articulated the simple question, "Who is Christ for us today?"

- In brief: "Individualization, breaking with tradition, as well as a growing cultural and religious pluralism have, in our day, led to a crisis in confessing Christ [Christusbekenntnis] which is more deeply disturbing than the questioning of the church's Christology that was part of the radical biblical criticism of the Enlightenment and the 'life of Jesus research.'"[4]

---

1. See Kühn, *Christologie*, 39–45, in this interesting context.
2. See also Dietrich Ritschl's comments in Ritschl and Hailer, *Diesseits und Jenseits der Worte: Grundkurs Christliche Theologie*, 88 (hereafter cited as D. Ritschl, *Grundkurs*).
3. See my reflections in Wüstenberg, "Bonhoeffer 'Revisited,'" 129–40.
4. Hoping, *Einführung in die Christologie*, 9.

IS A CHRISTOLOGY AT ALL POSSIBLE?

In light of this situation, how does one respond to those students at the party when they ask the famous "why" question? Does one say:

- That the doctrine of Jesus Christ is the "core of any Christian theology"?[5]
- That it presents "the *proprium* of the Christian understanding of God"?[6]
- That one can find in Christology a *compendium theologiae* (Thomas of Aquinas), or a summary of all theology?
- That talk of Jesus Christ always means *more* than making reference to the historical person of Jesus of Nazareth and that the title of Christ expresses the meaning of the saving significance of Jesus in the context of the eschatological expectations of Israel and of Jesus as none other than the Holy One of Israel?[7]

All is correct, all is important—but does it resonate with the line of questioning described above? In this part of the world, apparently not—or at least not in this *de*contextualized form. I myself cannot recall that either assertive statements or dogmatic explanations were ever able to ignite a living dialogue. Rather, experience teaches caution. One must also be ready for anti-Judaistic lapses of a dialogue partner when the discussion shifts to the Holy One of Israel. Often, one can consider oneself fortunate when the discussion moves on to an exchange concerning personal, existential experiences. Not infrequently, a feeling that one's soul has been stripped naked, and even shame, remains: the subject of God is embarrassing because in Christian theology it necessarily has something to do with Jesus Christ. Is this feeling perhaps a first indication of what almost every Christology refers to as the Pauline *skandalon*?

It is interesting that we don't encounter the "why" question in other parts of the world. I have experienced this myself in South Africa and America where, when I say that I am engaged in the study of Christian religion or theology, people express interest with amazing regularity. There is nothing in their response that would seem

---

5. Pannenberg, *Grundzüge der Christologie*, 13.
6. Hoping, *Einführung in die Christologie*, 9.
7. See Marquardt, *Das christliche Bekenntnis zu Jesus, dem Juden*.

to require a justification, followed by such questions as "Why are you doing that?" or "Aren't you interested in anything else?" Rather, there is empathetic curiosity: "Interesting—tell me more!" Even in England, one is surprised to find the names of streets and colleges in Cambridge that bear semblance to quite dogmatic contents in such a modern, secular university city: "Trinity College," "Jesus Lane," etc. (Admittedly, as one will quickly discover in discussions with theologians, there is little reason for euphoria, rather reminiscences of former days—but even so!)

Of course there is an overlap of church, society, and politics![8] At these junctures, churches are more like "places of religious awareness" than traditional places of worship. In many of them there is a revival of interest in religion (or better yet, of something diffuse "religious")[9] which, however, has little to do with any explicit confession of Jesus Christ. I am thinking, for instance, of grief services that are filled to overflowing after a terrorist attack or a natural disaster (which of course have to do with a search for peace and comfort in something transcendent or in a familiar ritual). I could also point here to certain academic events in which, when invited to speak, one now has to think twice about grounding social-ethical views in Christology.

Isn't Bonhoeffer's observation still very timely: that we have come to a time in which we must speak *etsi deus non daretur* (as if there were no God) about anything relevant? Have values of import not been passed on for a long time *as if there were no God*? Must we not ask today, as Dietrich Bonhoeffer did in 1944 in his prison cell in Berlin-Tegel, who Jesus Christ actually is for us today?

Is all this only a problem of context, a problem of Western society? I think the problem lies deeper—in our intellectual histories and traditions. There is much more behind it, which, in turn, begs the analytical question, "Why is this so?" How can we speak theologically about Jesus today—in the face of the implicit questions and arguments inherited from tradition? In short: Who is Jesus Christ for us today?

---

8. Sociologists may excuse here my lack of differentiation.

9. See the lovely observations of the religious sociologist Peter L. Berger on this phenomenon in his commentary on the apostles in chapter 10 of his *Questions of Faith*.

IS A CHRISTOLOGY AT ALL POSSIBLE?

Five Arguments Opposing the Message of Jesus as the Christ: Religious Pluralism, Faith in Science, Spiritualism, Humanism, and Feminism

There is much to support the view that in today's world one cannot develop a doctrine of Jesus Christ without reflecting today's intellectual history—at least to some extent—since Jesus Christ would have to be articulated in this context. We must therefore first address objections from intellectual-historical, social-critical, interreligious, and other perspectives: the secularization of the attitude of life, the experience of a variety of religious movements, and a completely historically defined consciousness of truth.

The key terms are these: religious pluralism, faith in science, spiritualism, humanism, and feminism. In view of the implicit questions related to these different perspectives, I would like here to lay out five objections to Christology. Although they stem from different intellectual contexts, they nowadays regulate almost every discussion about Jesus Christ (even if, for the most part, they remain hidden). As a result, they challenge in different ways traditional doctrine, the faith of Christian people, and the preaching of the church:

- The tolerance objection: does faith in Jesus Christ necessarily lead to intolerance?
- The historical-intellectual objection: is faith in Jesus Christ only a phantasm for religious fanatics?
- The spiritual-existential objection: is Christology something other than a dead letter and cold belief in dogma?
- The humanistic-enlightened objection: how can a loving God allow the death of his son in such a gruesome drama?
- The feminist-liberation theology objection: how can the man Jesus redeem?

These objections and the ideas behind them will be analyzed and discussed in the following pages. Finally, the challenge will be addressed of how it is still possible today to speak theologically about Jesus Christ. The methodology is analytical to the extent that it will explicate the "implied axioms" (Dietrich Ritschl) that are included in the majority of the encountered objections. Afterwards, we will ask how appropriate speech of Jesus Christ is possible under the conditions of these objections. One could also say along with Foucault that what follows is a "counter discourse" (*Gegendiskurs*)!

First, I will discuss current objections from the area of *religious pluralism*, as well as in light of Jewish-Christian conversations. These fundamental questions regarding the explication of Jesus Christ's meaning for Christian faith essentially correspond to the fundamental questions from the feminist perspective. They range from objections regarding tolerance within the framework of the pluralism debate, to feminist objections about the alleged "un-usability" of the Christology of the ancient church for liberation theology. Within this framework, three "classical" questions regarding the "historical Jesus" (Christology as "phantasm for religious fanatics"), the mystery of the person of Jesus (church council decisions as "cold dogmatic faith"), and his "work" (reconciliation as a "gruesome drama") will be discussed.

In surveying all of these objections, it is important to differentiate strictly between the questions that are answered by the ancient church's development of the teachings of Jesus Christ and the questions that are asked today. The latter are usually different and thus cannot be answered by doctrines developed by the ancient church. However, the fact that there are some surprising similarities is accurately described by Dietrich Ritschl in the following: "The modern Christians of the twenty-first century have not a little in common with those of the second and third centuries: the minority situation of the churches, an exceedingly complex cultural and religious pluralism, the similarity between the gnosis of the time and today's renewed interest in religiosity, in esoteric and in the occult, an irritating shift of values in ethics and morality, superpowers and dependent countries, colonized nations, etc."[10] Thus, it is indeed very worthwhile to engage in an intellectual and historical journey of discovery into the heights and depths of the doctrine of Jesus Christ.

---

10. D. Ritschl, *Grundkurs*, 71.

2

Accepting the Challenges

Christology in a Pluralistic World of Equally Valid Options

Does Faith in Jesus Christ Necessarily Lead to Intolerance?

Whoever talks about Jesus with people of other faiths, or with those who are nonreligious, is sooner or later confronted with the question of whether or not there are *absoluta*—that is, claims to exclusivity—anymore and how the Christian faith relates to this. Doesn't Christianity always strive for *absoluta*? Does a look into history tell us something else? Can we still assume any *absoluta* in today's religious worship of God? John Hick and other representatives of the *pluralistic theology of religion*, such as Paul Knitter,[1] ask these questions and advise caution: all religions can only claim a relative knowledge of God. In general, any claim to finality should be dismissed and a general "parting with principles" (O. Marquardt[2]) ought to take place. In addition, the political implications of religious claims to exclusivity should be considered: doesn't every claim to the absolute lead necessarily to fundamentalism and consequently to ideological rigidity, something that seems obvious in the aftermath of September 11, 2001? A Christology that teaches the exclusivity of salvation through Jesus Christ would seem to be problematic in this

---

1. See for example Knitter, *One Earth, Many Religions: Multifaith Dialogue and Global Responsibility*.

2. Cf. O. Marquardt, *Abschied vom Prinzipiellen: Philosophisch Studien*.

context. How then can traditional Christology, with its emphasis on a claim to exclusivity, remain in force in an age of new encounters with world religions? Doesn't Christology necessarily come off as intolerant? Won't exclusive statements from the New Testament (such as "No one comes to the Father but by me" [John 14:6]) make dialogue with other religions impossible? Christology seems not only to lack the capacity for interreligious dialogue, such as with Islam, but also for dialogue between Jews and Christians. Christology even looks like the "other side of anti-Judaism" (R. Ruether[3]) and anti-Judaism is perceived as the "left hand of Christology" (G. Baum[4]). Would the confession of Christ rob "the Jewish people . . . of one of their own central symbols" (P. van Buren[5])?

The Challenge of Religious Pluralism

It cannot to be overlooked that the present age is characterized by a radical pluralism[6] that regards any categorical claim to truth as questionable. The result of this is that frequently, and under these conditions, religion only appears to provide relative answers to the question of death and life. It has been often suggested that today's situation is remarkably similar to the situation of Christianity during the golden age of the Roman Empire.[7] Then, much like today, faith in the God of the Bible was not something one could assume, in contrast to later periods of Christian history. Yet, today's religious pluralism appears in many respects to go well beyond the intellectual historical situation of that ancient period—both in terms of its intensity and in terms of its scale. This phenomenon results from the

---

3. See Ruether, *Nächstenliebe und Brudermord: Die theologischen Wurzeln des Antisemitismus*, 229. (English: *Faith and Fratricide: The Theological Roots of Anti-semitism*.)

4. By Gregory Baum while teaching in Montréal, cited by Ruether, *Nächstenliebe*, 19.

5. van Buren, *Christ in Context*, 10.

6. On the concept of an evangelical theological discussion, see Herms, "Pluralismus aus Prinzip"; Härle, "Aus dem Heilgen Geist"; Schwöbel, *Christlicher Glaube im Pluralismus*, esp. 1–24.

7. Cf. D. Ritschl, *Grundkurs*, 71; Schwöbel, *Christlicher Glaube im Pluralismus*, 1–60.

powerful forces of modernity, a fact that is underscored by sociologist of religion Peter L. Berger. These forces include:

> urbanization and migration, throwing people with the most diverse backgrounds into close proximity with each other, together with mass literacy and the media of mass communication, which allows access to the beliefs and values of people virtually everywhere. Thus every major bookstore in Europe and America, and increasingly elsewhere, contains inexpensive books giving reasonably reliable information about the major religious traditions of human history. And the electronic media, capped by the Internet, provide even easier access to every conceivable religious phenomenon. This situation has thrown down a serious challenge to every institution with an absolute truth claim.[8]

The religio-sociological positioning of the claim to exclusivity within institutions as, for instance, the church as undertaken by Peter L. Berger has yet to be challenged from a Christian theological perspective. The fact is that Christology changes the theological terrain markedly. One could very simply say: the common ground of the three largest mono-theistic traditions has been abandoned, and the specifically Christian ground accessed. One has arrived at the *skandalon* of the Christian faith: namely, the emphasis on faith *in the person and work of Jesus Christ*. From the Jewish or Muslim point of view, this comes close to or even equals blasphemy against *the one* God. And from the vantage point of Southern or East Asian traditions, it is an expression of a completely narrow, quasi-local patriotic particularism.

The Absoluteness of Christ and the Plurality of Religion

The problem outlined in the "tolerance objection" is one that I would like to phrase as the following question: How can we think about, discuss, and teach about Jesus of Nazareth so that, on the one hand, the universality of his claim to truth remains intact while, on the other hand, other founders of religion and other forms of faith—especially

---

8. Berger, *Questions of Faith*, 14–15.

the Jewish faith—are not degraded in principle and replaced, their claim either relativized or even dismissed and branded as unbelief? A sufficient theological answer to this question is anything but simple. It would be far simpler to relativize or moralize faith, whereby one would have to let go of what one holds to be absolute, or tries to discover a common moral reference point of the religions.

First of all, it is remarkable that the "tolerance objection" is nothing new. The issue has been around since Lessing's "Nathan the Wise," which, in its famous fable of the three rings, relativizes the truth claims of Judaism, Islam, and Christianity. A certain position on the content of religion lies behind this story: namely, that faith in the one God is an essentially moral orientation.[9] Accordingly, under these conditions, all religions are very much "compatible."

Since Lessing, much has been thought about the question of the "absoluteness of the Christian faith": for instance, by contrasting Lessing's moral thesis of equality with a hierarchical model, the highest form of which is represented by Christianity (Troeltsch); or by setting Lessing against the widespread assumption in early dialectical theology that the Christian faith witnesses to the lack of truth of the other religions (Barth); or, finally, by proposing a "pluralistic theory of religion" (Hick), which essentially states that God's being, as revealed in Jesus, is equally expressed by different religions and pieties so that the different religions can participate in each other's wealth.

We will return to these models later. They each contain a different approach to pluralism. At this point, however, it is important to maintain that the development just outlined contains an obvious affinity to our objection mentioned above. Especially among the educated, there is the increasingly widespread view that with regard to God and the religious worship of God there can no longer be any absolutes. Rather, there can only be approximations of appropriate ways of speaking about God. And, do not any claims to the absolute inevitably lead to ideological and political rigidity? Is it not more reasonable, and from a global perspective, more necessary, for the believers of the different religions to join together in order to develop

---

9. See Kuschel, *Jude, Christ und Muselmann vereinigt: Lessings "Nathan, der Weise"* as well as his recent *Juden, Christen, Muslime*.

a common ethic on the basis of one religious option, thus helping to define a consensus on the pressing questions of humanity?[10]

A doctrine of Jesus Christ, which is responsibly placed within the context of religious pluralism, is faced with challenges from different perspectives. On the one hand, there is the increasingly loud question of whether we shouldn't relinquish all exclusive assertions when we think, speak of, and teach about the person, message, and work of Jesus of Nazareth. On the other hand, the truth claim emerges ever more powerfully: If the Christian confession of Christ is bound from the beginning by the witness of the New Testament—indeed, if the biblical proclamation witnesses to Jesus as the way, the truth, and the life (cf. John 14:12)—then a pluralistic theory of religion is not immediately possible. The question remains: How can we speak about this Jesus of Nazareth in a way that doesn't slam doors shut, but makes possible an open dialogue? The way we speak about Jesus of Nazareth, particularly with regard to his relationship to God, defines how we can engage with other faiths. This includes concrete questions, such as under what conditions common prayer, common meditative practice, or common ethical actions are possible.

A Possible Solution: Tolerance as the Core of Christian Faith: "Pluralism from Faith"

There have been various approaches with regard to the starting point for an intellectual history of religion and the problem of religious plurality connected to it.[11] As the smallest common denominator, one may distinguish between an "exclusive," a "pluralistic-relativistic," or an "inclusive" approach. My own suggested solution will—after the discussion of the models mentioned—be tied to "positional pluralism" (Härle), also known as "pluralism from faith" (Schwöbel).

1. The "exclusive" approach is seldom represented in today's theology. In the theology of the twentieth century, support for this position was most prominently found in the early Karl Barth, whose

---

10. Küng, *Global Responsibility: In Search of a New World Ethic.*

11. Cf. the theological discussion of Eilert Herms, Wilfried Härle, and Christoph Schwöbel referred to above.

revelation-theological interpretation of Kant's epistemology regards the term revelation indeed as having an exclusively Christian content: if, for Kant, the *thing in itself* is at least not-knowable, and for the Neo-Kantians it is a mere delimiting concept, then Barth agrees, as he argues that *God in himself* cannot be known, unless God makes himself *known* first through revelation. God's self-impartation is completed solely in Jesus Christ. Thus, in order for Christianity to be defined as the "true religion"[12] (and to distinguish it from disbelief as well as from other religions), the Christian concept of revelation must be particularly emphasized. Accordingly, Bonhoeffer spoke of the revelation-positivism of Karl Barth.[13] However, these days there are very few theologians (mainly Americans) who still maintain a claim to exclusivity. Among them is the Lutheran theologian Carl Braaten, whose 1992 book carries the programmatic title *No Other Gospel! Christianity among the World's Religions*.[14]

Despite the sympathy that can be garnered for clear-cut positions (they are, in many respects, more interesting than many of the rigid ecumenical platitudes) one must also look at the other side: the more one seriously engages with other traditions, the more exclusivity loses plausibility. One inevitably learns from the insights into reality that other approaches contain. A radical exclusivity therefore threatens to create the impression "that the activity of God is limited to Christianity and that God is not present in other religions if God is not conveyed to them by the message of Christ." Christoph Schwöbel aptly states, "This conception is, however, not in accord with the confession of Christ."[15]

2. In the pluralistic-relativistic approach—the extreme counter position to exclusivity—there can be no final revelation of the divine absolute. Religion's answers to the questions of life and death can only be relative. *Religious pluralism* appears here not (only) as a

---

12. See Barth, *Church Dogmatics* I/2 (§ 17)

13. Cf. here my "Der Einwand des Offenbarungspositivismus. Was hat Bonhoeffer eigentlich an Barth kritisiert?"

14. Braaten is certainly no fanatic, but the chapter titles of his book indicate where he stands: "Absoluteness Is a Precondition of God's Lordship"; "Christ Alone Is the Heart of the Church's Message."

15. Schwöbel, *Christlicher Glaube im Pluralismus*, 202.

description of the empirical variety of co-existing or competing religious world views, but as a normative program of a theology of religions. The so-called "pluralistic theology of religion" emerges from this position. It is one branch of the "philosophy of religion," whose most prominent representative is John Hick.[16] Hick supports his pluralistic view of religion using Kant's distinction between the "thing in itself" and its "appearance," but draws an entirely different conclusion than does Karl Barth. Hick connects to Kant's transcendentalism the thesis that the transcendental (the absolute, the real) is essentially unknowable, and does not reveal itself ultimately to the world and in history. Even though not all religions fulfill their purpose in the same way and there are differences in their teachings, in principle they still provide equally valid answers to the questions of life and death.[17] For Hick, religions are various media of transcendence that serve people in a process that he describes as "soul-making"—leading them from an existence of "self-centeredness" to an existence of "reality-centeredness." They are different "soteriological paths" by which a person can find salvation, freedom, and final fulfillment.[18] Hick thus measures religions by their salvific effect and not by their teachings. The decisive criteria for evaluating religions like Hinduism, Buddhism, Christianity, Judaism, and Islam consequently lies in their soteriological effect. On the other hand, these assumptions lead to a relativizing of religious images and symbols, traditions, rites, and dogmas. Any final revelation of God in one human is rejected as irrational by Hick. The various images, ideas, and concepts of the transcendent are rather more like lenses through which the absolute can be viewed.

A pluralistic theology of religion acknowledges by means of "the divine" (the transcendent, the absolute, the real) something that overlaps with the plurality of different viewpoints and opinions. Accordingly, Jesus is reduced to a "catalyst" for our relationship to transcendence; a function that could be fulfilled by other religious figures as well. However, according to Christian understanding, Jesus

---

16. See Hick, *An Interpretation of Religion: Human Response to the Transcendent*.

17. Cf. also Schmidt-Leukel, "Das pluralistische Modell in der Theologie der Religionen."

18. Hick, *Interpretation of Religion*, 261f.

is more than just one among the many witnesses of the absolute. He is God's final revelation, God's self-imparting, the "historical absolute" (Schleiermacher) against which religious pluralism so vehemently fights. If faith in God is not to be the result of a mere subjective opinion, then Jesus Christ must be proclaimed as *the* way, *the* truth and *the* life for the world and therefore as "meaning in itself."[19] Thus, for the sake of its identity, Christianity must hold fast to the uniqueness of Christ. "A pluralistic de-absolutizing of Christology, which sees in Jesus of Nazareth merely one of the many faces of an eternal *logos*, merely one of its incarnations, but not God's ultimate revelation or the '*concretum universale*,' runs consequently into the danger of eliminating Christianity."[20] Christian theology can therefore not view religious pluralism from a pan-religious perspective, but only from the particular perspective of the Christian faith.

3. In contrast to the extremes of an exclusivist position, on the one hand, and the relative-pluralistic school, on the other, the inclusive position seeks to take into account that God is not only at work where the grace of God in Christ is known through faith and witnessed to in the proclamation of the message of the scriptures. Rather, all being in the world and all action in the world must be understood within the horizon of the activity of God. Inclusive views are found in Karl Rahner's concept of "anonymous Christianity,"[21] in Ernst Troeltsch's appreciation of the personal nature of the Christian religion as expressed in the view that Christianity is the only "presentation of the higher world as eternally valuable personal life that determines and forms everything else."[22] Finally, they are found in Paul Tillich's ontological notion of God as the "ground of being,"[23] as well as in his teachings on the spiritual community and the latent church, and,

---

19. See Menke, *Die Einzigkeit Jesu Christi im Horizont der Sinnfrage*, 75–110.

20. Hoping, *Einführung in die Christologie*, 18.

21. For a recent investigation, see Conway, *The Anonymous Christian—A Relativised Christianity?*

22. Cf. Troeltsch, *Die Absolutheit des Christentums und die Religionsgeschichte* (1902/191) 195. (English: *The Absoluteness of Christianity and the History of Religions*.)

23. Cf. Tillich, *Systematic Theology*.

under slightly different preconditions, the late Karl Barth's so-called "doctrine of the lights."[24]

Much more could be said in detail about each of these positions, yet at this juncture two points will have to suffice: on the one hand, it is clear that the positions outlined so far offer options that, at least in practice, are rather unusable in terms of the current pluralism debate and its attending interreligious dialogue. To exemplify the issue: who would seriously want to enter into a dialogue with Muslims in the Berlin district of Neukölln with the concept of "anonymous Christianity" or with the idea of God as the "ground of all being"? Or, indeed, apply these concepts by declaring them to be "anonymous" adherents of their own religious belief? Doubtless, questions regarding interreligious practices require other theological concepts that would allow one to speak of Jesus of Nazareth in such a way that other founders of religions and other forms of faiths are neither overwhelmed nor replaced, their claims not relativized or disqualified by Christ. On the other hand, Peter L. Berger[25] has recently pointed to the potential that is contained in the insights of Ernst Troeltsch. Berger uses the process of exclusion: the fact that God uniquely revealed himself to Israel and that all that followed in the subsequent centuries arose from this revelation does not mean, however, that one has "to deny *a priori* that God may have revealed himself at other times and in other places." To draw boundary lines on God's revelation, as is done in the exclusive approach, is dangerous and something against which Troeltsch has already warned. As a result, Berger now suggests, we should "remain open to that which might come to us from other traditions."

With regard to his premise, Berger's argument contains an essential contribution to the understanding of the Christian faith within religious pluralism. However, in my opinion, he goes too far as his revelation-theological optimistic conclusion of "remaining open to that which might possibly come to us from other religions," is concerned. Wouldn't it be better just to stay with gratitude? To be thankful for what has been given to us in this Judeo-Christian tradition without excluding the possibility that God could also have

---

24. See *Church Dogmatics* IV/3, first half.
25. See (also in the subsequent citations) Berger, *Questions of Faith*, 30ff.

revealed himself to other peoples in other ways? Indeed, is it not the case that the call for tolerance by the Christian faith rests precisely on the insight that only God can create faith and therefore the faith of others (as one's own) is beyond the grasp of human activity? "Faith is given, not made. This view of how religious certainty arises is, according to the Christian conception, true not only for Christians, but for all people, and it is true not only for the formation of the certainty of faith, but for any kind of certainty. This is the foundation of the freedom of the conscience, which was profiled in the Reformation in its protest against the claims of both ecclesiastic and worldly authority that wanted to bind the conscience to existing teachings."[26] If, in good Reformation tradition, faith is understood as the activity of God, then freedom and tolerance are included as well; indeed they are founded on the same foundation. Respect for other faiths thus exists in a corresponding relationship to the essence of Christian faith. "Tolerance from faith" is what Tübingen theologian Christoph Schwöbel[27] calls this insight, which constructively replaces the normative pluralism position of a theory of religion (Hick, Knitter) with that of a "positional pluralism" (Härle),[28] while it allows at the same time moments of truth of the inclusive position to remain. The idea of tolerance results from the christological conviction that faith is God's work and that, because it is inherently not at our disposition, no one can be coerced into it.

4. The position of "positional pluralism" makes possible a connection to the tension-rich relationship between absoluteness and relativism. "For the Christian faith, the absolute is only God, whose being is truth. All truth, where ever it is found, is strictly relative to the truth which is God."[29] Therefore, the character of absoluteness must not be transferred onto the institutions of religion (its educational system, its cultic practice, or the order of its offices). To speak of the absoluteness of Christianity (or of its "claim to absoluteness") not only inhibits dialogue from a practical point of view, it is theologically

---

26. Schwöbel, *Christlicher Glaube im Pluralismus*, 232.
27. Ibid., 18–21; 217–43.
28. Cf. Härle, "Aus dem Heiligen Geist."
29. Schwöbel, *Christlicher Glaube im Pluralismus*, 233. Following citation ibid., 234.

simply wrong. "The absolute authority of God's revelation which creates certainty is not transferrable to the various institutional and personal forms of revelatory testimony." Contrary to the pluralistic model of the theology of religion, Christian faith, according to its own self-understanding, does not choose "its" own truth, but is already chosen "by it." It has made itself accessible, without being "at one's disposal" (which can lead to fundamentalism).[30] This view "inward" to the innermost core of Christian faith correlates "outward" to the cosmic width of the Christian concept of reconciliation. It corresponds to the moments of truth of the inclusive positions, in which biblical indications of the universality of the Christ-event were to be recovered. These moments of truth include, in my view, both a political-cosmic and an interreligious aspect, particularly in the relationship between Judaism and Christianity. (With regard to other religions I have already voiced my agreement with Troeltsch's basic notion of inclusiveness, namely, that it is always dangerous to place limits on God's revelation. The possibility that God has made himself known to other peoples at other times cannot be excluded from the Christian point of view. For the Christian-Jewish relationship, however, this reference is not sufficient.)

Leipzig theologian Ulrich Kühn points to the cosmic aspect of universal reconciliation: where "the whole world belongs to the *logos*" (John 1:11), "the entire events of the world come into the light of the miracle of the incarnation. Stated in another way, God is the one who from eternity wanted to become human in Christ, for which reason the creation of the world already stands under the sign of God's covenant with the world."[31] The political aspect of the universal idea of reconciliation is something that I have already discussed in another book.[32] We may, and indeed should, search for "signs of transcendence" (P. L. Berger) of the Christian concept of reconcilia-

---

30. Fundamentalism as a reaction to a perceived threat to one's identity via the undermining of religious truth claims should be met from the perspective of a "pluralism from faith" by searching for the sources of tolerance in one's own religious traditions. "Only through a deeper confrontation with the richness of religious traditions is fundamentalism revealed as an impoverished caricature of religion, as the reflection of secularism in the medium of religion." Schwöbel, *Christlicher Glaube im Pluralismus*, 227.

31. Kühn, *Christologie*, 328f.

32. Wüstenberg, *The Political Dimension of Reconciliation*.

tion in the midst of political reality. And we may understand certain moments of peace-making (whether in the South African Truth Commission or elsewhere) in Christian terms but must not hold up this understanding in an exclusive way as a model of interpretation for others, especially for non-Christians. In spite (or better: because) of the Christian positioning, there must always be as a matter of principle an openness to different interpretations.

Thus, while on the one hand it is correct "that the reconciliation of the world with God that appeared in and was effected by Christ certainly demands a band of those who knowingly accept this reconciliation, actualize it in their lives and are united together with the congregation of those, to whom the worshipful celebration of this reconciliation is central. Yet on the other hand we may speak of a ray of hope that lights up the entire world, which here and there on earth—even where the name of Jesus Christ is not spoken—lets islands of newness and salutary life become reality in the world. It is then up to Christians to look for these signs and to recognize them and extend the hand of reconciliation to people of other faiths, in order to walk with each other the way of peace, 'which passes all understanding' (Phil 4:7)."[33]

In light of this statement, it is possible to formulate criteria for an Israel-affirming Christology in order at least to hint at the Judeo-Christian dimension.[34] This includes full acknowledgment of the Jewishness of Jesus, the development of a Christology that incorporates the messianic hopes of the people of Israel, as well as—in reference to Romans 11—the unqualified affirmation of the abiding election of the people of Israel. The last criterion, especially, according to which the special election of Israel is not a "perfektum"—a matter of the past—has played a central role in the Jewish-Christian dialogue from Karl Barth to Helmut Gollwitzer, and from Friedrich-Wilhelm Marquardt to Peter von der Osten-Sacken and Michael Weinrich, and has been appreciated also from the Jewish side.[35]

---

33. Kühn, *Christologie*, 329.

34. See the important ideas of Hoping, *Einführung in die Christologie*, 147ff.

35. See the positive recognition of Christian efforts from a Jewish perspective in the document *Dabru Emet*, and the constructive discussion of Kampling and Weinrich, *Dabru Emet—Redet Wahrheit*.

Accepting the Challenge of "Pluralism": The Ability for Dialogue "from the Inside" Out

In view of the charge of intolerance, how can we speak theologically about Jesus? Must not Christology necessarily be freed of all absolutes (J. Hick)? How else could it hold its own in an age of new encounters between world religions? Doesn't Christology *eo ipso* lack the ability for interreligious dialogue (such as with Islam), as well as for Judeo-Christian dialogue?

A Note of Encouragement

- Whoever accuses Christology as a matter of principle of lacking the ability for dialogue formally fails to note that the question of Jesus Christ is raised in a variety of ways outside the Christian space: Christology always exists, at least externally, "in dialogue"—in dialogue with other religions (one may think of the view of Jesus among Jewish thinkers, like Buber, as well as in Islam, Hinduism, and Buddhism), in dialogue with the philosophers of the twentieth century (one may think of the philosophical Christology of Tilliette, the existential-philosophical interpretation of Jesus by Karl Jasper, or the Marxist reception of Ernst Bloch and Milan Machovec), and in dialogue with contemporary literature.[36] The discovery of Jesus of Nazareth in other religions, in philosophy, as well as in contemporary literature underscores how reflective people today are affected by the person of Jesus.

- The objections from culture-theoretical pluralism against "Christianity's claim to absoluteness" cannot be answered either by relativism or with moralizing. Neither the moral equalization of religions (Lessing), nor the de-absolutizing of Christology (Hick) prove to be a viable path. The following holds true for both: being worthy of moral admiration is no criterion for truth; and even Jesus of Nazareth cannot be reduced to a moral teacher without the loss of christological substance. Furthermore, to treat Jesus

---

36. Compare the overview of Kuschel, *Jesus im Spiegel der Weltliteratur*, 11–36.

as a "model of true humaneness"[37] contributes little to interreligious dialogue, "when it is established *a priori* that only the fruits, yet not their roots in faith, are considered significant for ethical orientation."[38] It is these roots of Christian faith, however, that open up a genuine access to interreligious dialogue, namely in the form of tolerance that is vouched for by faith: faith itself is a gift and therefore not an absolute; for the Christian faith, only God, whose very being is truth, is absolute. Thus, all truth, wherever it is found, exists relative to this truth. There is therefore no claim to absoluteness *on the part of Christianity* that one should have to defend on theological grounds.

- The biblical (Judeo-Christian) tradition has had especially great respect for the worth and dignity of the human being, and not only regarding questions of morality. Christology particularly underscores an "ontological antiphony" (P. L. Berger) between the personality of God and that of human beings which, according to Luther, consists of the fact that humans exist as long as God continues turning toward them. The fact that faith in Jesus Christ is not owed to itself but rather to God establishes a way of entry to religious pluralism "from the inside," "out of its very substance." The constitution of faith is beyond our disposition:[39] this is where, on the one hand, the freedom—founded in faith—from any institutions or authorities has its roots. On the other hand, it is the ground on which Christian faith must renounce imposing itself on others. Certainty of truth cannot be prescribed for others.

- In light of these considerations, Christian faith cannot exclude the possibility that God has revealed himself to other peoples in other ways. What is true for the Judeo-Christian dialogue is also true for a dialogue with other religions: for the Christian faith, the evidence of the universality of the truth of faith in Jesus of Nazareth is a matter of eschatological hope. Whoever believes, knows therefore that this faith is a gift. And *this is why* one can enter into interreligious dialogue in a truly *tolerant* way.[40]

---

37. Hick, *Myth of God Incarnate*, 188.
38. Schwöbel, *Christlicher Glaube im Pluralismus*, 191.
39. For the constitutional conditions of faith, see Härle, *Dogmatik*, 69ff.
40. This concept of tolerance, according to which, on the basis of

ACCEPTING THE CHALLENGES

- Wherever Christology is said to be the "obverse side of anti-Judaism" (Ruether) or anti-Judaism the "left hand of Christology" (Baum), and where it is even claimed that the confession of Christ "robs the Jewish people one of its own central symbols" (van Buren), one still stands on the ground of the theory of supercession: namely, the church replaces Israel (OT=promise; NT=fulfillment). Here, one needs to remember that Jewish-Christian dialogue has meanwhile moved forward considerably (recently, for instance, with the discussion of "Dabru Emet"). The "yes" to Jesus, the Christ, is in itself not finished. Rather, it remains open to the messianic future of Jesus.[41]

- Among the religions, Judaism enjoys a special place in relation to Christianity. The God who meets us in Jesus of Nazareth is the God of Israel and not some kind of "second God." A good knowledge of the Christology of the early church can help bring an Israel-affirming Christology into dialogue: Jesus of Nazareth comes from Israel. Only the Jew Jesus is the Christ to the Christians. In this regard, it is clear why Jesus' "being Jewish" is theologically significant: "It cannot mean," says Karl Barth, "that we believe in Jesus Christ, who also happened to be an Israelite. . . . Here one must think very rigorously: Jesus Christ . . . was necessarily Jewish. . . . God became human in Jewish flesh. This fact is not to be overlooked, since it belongs to the concrete reality of God and his revelation."[42]

Reformation theology, tolerance can be gained from the faith unavailable to our disposition, is different from the perceptions that view tolerance as a virtue, which possibly includes the claim that only what is repudiated can be tolerated. Cf. to this the discussion in Forst, *Toleranz*. An overview of tolerance research is available in Wierlacher, *Kulturthema Toleranz*.

41. Cf. Moltmann, *Der Weg Jesu Christi. Christologie in messianischen Dimensionen*, 1989 (English: *The Way of Jesus Christ: Christology in Messianic Dimensions*).

42. Cited in Lapide and Rahner, *Heil von den Juden*, 57f.

3

Christology in a World of Progress and Historical Scholarship

Is the Matter of Jesus Only a Phantasm for Religious Fanatics?

From the modern historical perspective, it is not insignificant that the central point of reference of Christian faith, namely Jesus of Nazareth, does not stand the test of historical examination. Does this not mean that Christology is a pure "matter of faith," indeed a "phantasm" for religious fanatics? The historical reports about Jesus are challenged about their reliability. What makes us so sure that he actually lived? And if he lived—was his resurrection also "historical"? Was the grave really empty? Or does Christology have as its substance a nonverifiable claim of the first witness? How much "historical Jesus" does faith require so that everything doesn't turn into a "subjective matter of faith"? Must one not honestly admit (on account of the undermining brought about by historical scholarship) that faith itself already threatens to dissolve into pure subjectivity or spirituality, thus losing any connection to modern consciousness, which to a large extent is permeated by "earthly" historical research and its understanding of scholarship? Are evangelical circles not an eloquent manifestation of this trend? Does the Christian religion not look like the special room one retreats to on Sunday for a few hours, only to return later to one's real tasks?

What Do We Actually Know about Jesus and His Time?

"Historically, there are two facts that cannot be seriously contested: Jesus' crucifixion in Jerusalem, and the appearance of a 'rumor' spread there by several of his disciple that he appeared to them alive after his death."[1] These facts are said to have occurred around the year 30 CE, when for a brief period—from one to one and a half years—the Jew Jesus of Nazareth was active in Galilee. The period of Caesar Tiberius' reign was one of political and religious turmoil; social and religious differences divided groups of people and led to many conflicts; people responded to the Roman occupation with ever increasing opposition. During this period, people were looking to God to intervene with mighty acts: the rejected will be judged, the elect will be saved, and God will establish his reign. This hope was depicted in a great variety of ways. Jesus of Nazareth had proclaimed the nearness of this God. He worked as an itinerant preacher and told of the imminent coming of the reign of God. He spoke of the Son of Man, who would usher in the new world through judgment and salvation. He reached out to people irrespective of differences and accepted them unconditionally. He awakened courage and trust, and freed people to be themselves: through words, helpful deeds, examples, and the open communion of meals. Reaching out to people, taking part in their lives, whether weary and heavy-laden, humiliated and insulted, secure or well-fed—was this a testimony to the power and authority of God?

Jesus of Nazareth was said to be a human being of flesh and blood like "you and me" and yet completely different from how we human beings are otherwise. But no one wanted Jesus to be the way he was, not his family, nor his friends or his enemies, nor the leaders of his people or the state in which he lived. Jesus portrayed the full measure of humanity. He is the historical revelation of the humanity of God. At any rate, he was a human being in a way that we are not used to otherwise. May one presume that the reason for this is

---

1. Dalferth, "Volles Grab, leerer Glaube?" 384.

that in him God is continually and eternally near to human beings? If so, then Jesus' activity would be provocative: "Are you he who is to come? Or should we wait for another?" asked his disciples. Jesus referred to his actions and answered, "The blind see and the lame walk, lepers are healed and the deaf hear, the dead are raised and the Gospel is preached to the poor" (Matt 11:3–5).

Jesus gained disciples. They were mainly people of lowly estate and also included women. They accepted him and traveled with him. Jesus also garnered opponents that became his enemies. He provoked people; they opposed him and tried to do away with him. In Jerusalem he was arrested and interrogated, and after a short trial—the details of which are obscure—was sentenced to death by the Roman procurator and executed on a cross. The death of Jesus was the end of his "historical" work. We know very little about the behavior of his disciples at his death. A short time after his death it was said that Jesus was alive. This "rumor" (Dalferth) is historically accurate. Jesus was proved right, they said—he is not done with. Only a very small group of people dared to claim this: most of them were from the group of Jesus' followers from the earliest days. The conviction of this group can be historically ascertained. However, the *foundation* for this conviction is not something that can be determined using historical research. His disciples named it the "resurrection of Jesus from the dead." It gave rise to the conviction that the Jesus of Nazareth who had been killed, lives. Not much can be established about what happened there and how. The New Testament witness about Christ is grounded in the experience of the first witnesses and in the confession that Jesus of Nazareth rose from the dead.[2]

In Jesus of Nazareth, this confession of the early Christians connects what had been a widely expected eschatological hope in Judaism with Jesus of Nazareth. He becomes Jesus, the Christ. The

---

2. This knowledge refers to the event that Christians have described using the metaphor *arising,* i.e., *resurrection.* The image, taken from daily life, described waking up after a night's sleep and the activity of rising for the morning. In Jewish as well as in Greek thought, the metaphor of sleep was also used for death. In later Judaism it was connected with the idea of rising after the sleep of death. Whether only believers or all people were to hope in such a resurrection was a rather controversial topic in Judaism during the time of Jesus. In any case, the idea of a general resurrection of the dead to a new, eternal life is rooted in Jewish-eschatological hope.

designation of Jesus of Nazareth as Christ (Messiah, the Anointed) is of special significance because this "royal title" seems to signal the Jewish-Christian difference. This differentiation is grounded already in the New Testament also and specifically in the title for Christ (cf. Mark 14:61). Since according to Jewish understanding, the coming Messiah would establish ultimate peace on earth, it would seem abundantly clear that Jesus could not be the Messiah. However, one must also keep in mind that Jewish conceptions of the Messiah at that time did not anticipate exclusively or even primarily a real ruler, but the one who as the Anointed is uniquely connected to God so as to bring about salvation. Precisely this unique relationship to God is, however, what the early Christian faith saw as realized in Jesus. It is the singular connection to the one God, who in Jesus faces human beings and through Jesus calls them to himself and makes them his own. And this image of Christ is shaped above all by the suffering that he endured. The Messiah that the Christian faith sees in Jesus and confesses is the Messiah in his utterly un-messianic life, a life that is so completely without external luster. Thus, for the post-Easter faith, Jesus is the One in whom God definitely and unsurpassably comes to humans and in which his coming now is a sign of his coming again—his ultimate future (cf. Acts 1:11). The latter once again links the hope of Christians and Jews. Until then, however, this Jesus Christ is sent to all people, and available also for Israel.

That "Jesus" and "Christ" are fused into a proper name already in the New Testament points to a noteworthy hermeneutic accomplishment in early Christian proclamation, namely, the christological transformation of the experience of Jesus of Nazareth to the confession of Jesus as the Christ. This confession was expressed at that time in various ways just as it is today: as a firm formula in baptism and worship, as well as in the language of witness and conversation. It defined and defines the actions of those who confess. In its many various forms this post-Easter confession seeks to do only one thing, namely, to make Jesus of Nazareth known as the ultimate, decisive authority to come to understand him and to help others to do so as well. This involved trying to show the hopes of the Jews to the broken, the powerful God to the powerless. It meant seeking to show the crucified criminal to be the ultimate, decisive authority, and setting the misery (*Unheil*) of death against the well-being (*Heil*) of true life, and accidental events happening at the margins of world against the necessity that governs everyone. In all this the theory of this confession had to be brought together with the practice of those confessing in such a way that it did justice equally to the Jesus spoken of and the people spoken to.

Do We Really Know about Jesus What We Think We Know? (History and Faith)

In the previous summary, we outlined the route taken from an encounter with Jesus of Nazareth to the confession of the early Christian community that this Jesus is the Christ. The historical pivot points were the cross and the "rumor" (Dalferth) of the resurrection. We will now go one step further and problematize the identity of the Christ of faith in relation to the historical Jesus. Is the resurrected Christ, the Lord to whom the New Testament gives witness, recognizably the same as the earthly Jesus of Nazareth, the messenger of the kingdom of God, who was tried and condemned to death on account of his message? This question was already there at the beginning of Christian history—it was already there during Jesus' lifetime when he asked his disciples, "Who do you say that I am?" In many respects this is still the key question. This question became more intense when modern historical scholarship focused its critical methodology on the New Testament. The problems presented by historical scholarship caused a crisis of faith in Christian communities. Does Christology have to do with scholarly indefensible assumptions that one is simply asked to believe? Is Christology, the teaching about Jesus Christ, perhaps not at all a scholarly-historial teaching but, rather, a pure matter of faith, much like a structure of *Credenda* (things to be believed)? This is at least what Hermann Reimarus claimed; he was not a theologian but a professor of oriental languages in Hamburg. In 1778, Lessing published one of his books, titled *The Purpose of Jesus and His Disciples*. Here Reimarus suggested that Jesus was a failed political prophet who was subsequently executed as such by Roman officials. His body was then stolen from the grave by his disciples, who built a myth around the dead man. Reimarus' thesis is this: Jesus was a teacher who taught a religion oriented towards practical action and, therefore, not one with new secrets or articles of faith, but all kinds of moral teachings and duties of life. He also preached the kingdom of God. At the end, however, he despaired; and his disciples stole him from the grave, claiming that he was resurrected.

According to Reimarus, Christianity ought to be understood as the endless reweaving of this myth. This was clearly a radical attempt at unmasking Christianity and with it its Christology as a purely subjective affair of faith. However, many details of Reimarus' approach are not tenable in view of later research. Nevertheless, he is still important; not least because he emphatically emphasized the difference between the "historical Jesus" and the "Christ of faith."

Historical research into the New Testament experienced an upsurge during the entire nineteenth century, primarily within Protestant institutions and in the context of so-called liberal theology. People wanted to get down to the truth of the "historical" Jesus. An additional focal point of this effort was the attempt to free Christology from church dogma. This served the purpose of creating an historical diagram of the life of Jesus without having to advocate any faith assumptions. This effort did not serve—as was the case with Reimarus—the basic goal of unmasking, but rather was a response to the criticism of various rigid, "dogmatic" conceptions. The intention was to give faith a solid historical foundation, even if it meant that many of the opinions held by Protestantism had to be abandoned. Today, this project is typically called the *old* or the *first search for the historical Jesus*. During this period there were, of course, many competing views. Nevertheless, a wide consensus developed that the— so-called—orthodox conceptions of Jesus cannot count on being supported by historical scholarship. The theologian Martin Kähler went well beyond this consensus in his influential work.[3] Kähler argued that we cannot know the historical Jesus at all, because all of the New Testament accounts about him serve the message of the Christ of faith. That is why faith has to be independent of the results of historical research.

The problem that emerges in the scholarly-historical critique but without protective support is this: all the relevant texts of the New Testament are expressions of faith in Jesus as the Christ. Particularly

3. See Kähler, *The So-Called Historical Jesus and the Historical Biblical Christ*.

the Gospels are not exercises in "objective" historical erudition because they manifest specific, and by no means unified, theological viewpoints. The problem of the so-called historical Jesus therefore rests in this simple issue: the major portion of what we know as the New Testament came into being after the life of Jesus. It is, so to speak, written "backwards" in time from the perspective of those who believed in the resurrection of Jesus from the dead; that is, it is written from the perspective of Easter. Indeed, the Gospels, which tell so vividly of the life, works, sufferings, death, and resurrection of Jesus of Nazareth, emerged only after the letters of Paul. In any case, we are being enlightened that the reality is not at all as one might be inclined to deduce from a naive reading of the Gospels, that someone traveled with Jesus much like a reporter, so that with the Gospels we hold a historical travel diary in our hands. On the contrary, the sources are very meagre. This being the case, upon what can faith be built if not upon the "historical Jesus"?

A Possible Solution:
"We Don't Know Christ Anymore in the Flesh"

At least four attempts have been made to solve the previously outlined problem of faith and history. First, the area of the historical Jesus itself: The intention was to detach the presumably untenable assumptions of faith from Jesus of Nazareth whose life it was thought could be reconstructed historically. This attempt presented itself in the form of modern "scholarship," in order to counter the objection that the substance of Christology consists in essence of historically untenable facts. Thus, scholarly untenable faith could be given an "historical scholarly" foundation and Christology could then be uncoupled from the historical Jesus. Such a "Jesuology" no longer appears to be a historically untenable matter of faith; rather, the life of Jesus could now be open to reconstruction using the means of historical research. Every theologian worth his salt wrote a "life of Jesus." The final expression of the life-of-Jesus research, which tried to resolve the tension between history and faith one-sidedly in favor of history, was written by the theologian, and later medical doctor, Albert Schweitzer. In his *Quest of the Historical Jesus* (as the second edition of his book of 1906 is titled), Schweitzer portrayed in beautiful literary and theologically apt fashion how the various representations of the "life of Jesus" reflected the life and the proclivities of their various authors rather than presenting a serious scholarly approach to the historical Jesus of Nazareth. Schweitzer's highly influential book uncovered theology's naïve adaptation to modern liberal thought, which above all misrepresented the historical Jesus by moralizing his message. Jesus was not a teacher of morality but an eschatological preacher who saw both the end of the world and the imminent establishment of the reign of God. According to Schweitzer, the "spiritual" Jesus is of vital importance for the twentieth century. In the final analysis, this takes Schweitzer back to Reimarus's dichotomy of faith and history. (At this juncture it is worth mentioning that among other positions of intellectual history, a certain revival of the life-of-Jesus position can be seen in recent Anglo-Saxon discussions, a phenomenon that we have already mentioned. John Hick, for example, maintained that the incarnation is no longer to be considered a matter of faith since it belongs historically to a later tradition and, correspondingly, is not tenable in scholarship.[4])

Next to the attempts to write a "life of Jesus" and Schweitzer's discussion of the problems related with them, a second attempt at a solution was offered at about the same time; it was rooted in the theological thought of Martin Kähler already referred to. Kähler not only doubted the *results* of the "life of Jesus research" but also its *assumptions*. According to his thesis, the New Testament does not ask about Jesus in the categories of history. Rather, it is much more a witness of faith that reflects the impact of Jesus on the people of his time. In short: it does not portray how Jesus was historically but how he impacted his environment. Faith in Jesus as the Christ necessarily belongs to that impact. The central impulse of Kähler's thesis bore fruit after the First World War, particularly in the so-called *dialectical theology* and the meaning it gave to the event of Easter. Karl Barth wrote that it would be downright wholesome for faith if historical research were removed from under its feet: "Whoever does not yet know ... that we *no* longer know Christ according to the flesh, should let the critical study of the Bible tell him so. The more radically he is

---

4. Hick, *The Myth of God Incarnate*.

frightened the better it is for him and for the matter involved."⁵ For Rudolf Bultmann, the pre-Easter proclamation of Jesus of Nazareth is at best a historical precondition of the post-Easter preaching of the congregation: "The message of Jesus is a precondition of the theology of the New Testament rather than a part of that theology itself."⁶

A third position modifies Bultmann's (and in part Barth's) approach and is advanced primarily by the Bultmann school. Here the question turns anew to the historical Jesus, but from the vantage point of Easter. For example, Ernst Käsemann stresses the theological significance of a reference back to the pre-Easter situation in the post-Easter interpretation of the *kerygma* by Bultmann. "The Easter faith was the foundation of the Christian *kerygma*, but was not the first and only source of its content."⁷ Thus faith relates to an experience outside of itself (*extra nos*)—a process that Käsemann thought was threatened by Bultmann's existential interpretation. An assumptionless, even neutral "scientific" question about the historical Jesus (as it was sought after by the liberal Jesus research), is excluded. Käsemann's "new question" concerning the historical Jesus is full of presuppositions and, setting out from Easter, the question searches rather and more profoundly for God's activity in Jesus of Nazareth.

Finally, a fourth position resolves the theological tension between history and faith in radical contrast to the attempt at a solution by the liberal Jesus research. As such, now it is not faith, but rather history that is abandoned. Irrespective of how the resurrection of Jesus took place historically, the only really important message is the one of reconciliation in its cosmic dimension. For Peter L. Berger,⁸ for example, it is inconsequential whether the disciples secretly took away Jesus' body and the women stood before "the empty tomb with amazement" or whether Jesus of Nazareth did not really die on the cross. For him it is conceivable "that Jesus revived and took off from wherever his unconscious body had been laid—and, who knows, lived quietly to an old age, having prudently given up any charismatic activities." According to Berger, these ideas would not destroy faith in

---

5. Thus, Karl Barth in Pkt. 14 responds to Adolf von Harnack, in "Die Christliche Welt 1923," cited in Rumscheidt, *Revelation and Theology*, 35.

6. Bultmann, *Theology of the New Testament*, 1:3 (translation altered).

7. Käsemann, "The Problem of the Historical Jesus" (1954).

8. Compare Berger, *Questions of Faith*. Subsequent citations ibid., 66–67.

the resurrection, since the cosmic event of the resurrection "was not and is not dependent on what really happened empirically."

While the fourth approach to a solution depends only slightly, or not at all, upon faith in the historical Jesus, the complete opposite is true for the first approach to a solution: all, or at least much, hinges on knowledge of the historical Jesus. Both positions appear to be equally difficult in their own way. In the first instance, the recommendation not to make faith dependent on the current state of historical research is obviously good. On the other hand, it must be asked of the fourth approach whether Jesus "without history" is not rather more suited to be a vehicle for ideology than a way to redemption. For it is true historically: "without the cross, faith hangs in the air historically speaking."[9] And it is true from a soteriological point of view that Jesus can only "truly" save people if he was "truly human."

That leaves the "middle" positions 2 and 3, whereby, as far as I can see, position 3 (albeit in diverse forms) is more or less acknowledged as the theological consensus. If one asks about the person of Jesus from the vantage point of Easter, then this question is connected to legitimate scholarly research on the historical Jesus without having to concede the view that faith is built upon verification of the historical words of Jesus. (That would also clearly be a somewhat "thin" foundation, since one may proceed from the conclusion that in the advanced reconstruction of the so-called "Q" source only a good dozen "reliable" sayings by Jesus are to be found.[10]) It is the

> character of the Christian faith that its defining point of reference is a person of history who is also an object of historical research. Because this is so, the historically verifiable dates are of theological significance in the sense that they offer the "material" in which faith "reads" God's activity for the salvation of the world. To this extent faith is always in the highest degree interested in the results of historical research. This faith looks backwards from the light of Easter to Jesus, to his way, his message, his death. In the light of Easter, faith affirms the claim of

---

9. Dahlferth, "Volles Grab, leerer Glaube?" 379.

10. A list of the verified authentic words of the "historical Jesus" can be found, for example, in Simonis, *Jesus Christus*, 103f.

the pre-Easter Jesus and sees in Jesus of Nazareth indeed God's saving activity.[11]

An Example: The Divine Origin of Jesus (Four Models)

Exegetical theology has shown by means of historical-critical research that the New Testament consists of numerous interwoven text-threads and that it mirrors a highly tangled history of tradition. The earlier assumption of the unity of the New Testament canon has proven itself to be a phantom unity. In the same measure, the variety, one may even say plurality, of contradistinctions has become increasingly more evident. Right from the start, theology has existed only in the form of theologies. The New Testament as the biblical basis for the witness of Jesus Christ also does not simply arrive at a unilinear conclusion about Jesus. Every more attentive reader of the New Testament scriptures very quickly arrives at the simple fact that there is no unified description of Jesus in them, no so-to-speak sure and always reproducible "normal picture" of Jesus. Even the original witnesses also portray Jesus differently: John differently than Paul, Peter differently than James. And just as theology existed from its very beginning only as theologies, so also Christology only as Christologies. We only need to take the question of the divine origin of Jesus as an example! How do we arrive at a description of Jesus as the Son of God? Where does the sonship of God come from? Mark presents a different model than Luke, and John's model is different compared to that of Mark and Luke. In his letters to the Romans, Paul asserts a central viewpoint that the other three (i.e., Mark, Luke, John) do not use as a basis for knowledge of the divine origin of Jesus, namely, the resurrection.

In summary, four models can be found in the New Testament: the installation in the sonship of God through the resurrection (Rom 1:4); the call to sonship through baptism (Mark 1:9-10); the birth of God's Son from the Virgin Mary (Matt 1/Luke 1); and the preexistence of the Son of God (John 1).[12]

---

11. Kühn, *Christologie*, 117f.
12. Compare also Härle, *Dogmatik*, 347ff.

The Installation in the Sonship of God through the Resurrection, according to Romans 1:4

For Paul, Jesus proved himself to be the Son of God through his death on the cross. The resurrection of Jesus Christ is thus the virtual seal of his witness. There is much to indicate that the title "Son of God" was first used for Jesus after the resurrection, that is, after Easter. Accordingly, Paul says "designated Son of God in power by his resurrection." In this theological perspective, the resurrection is the sealing of the proclamation and ministry of Jesus of Nazareth, as well as the final confirmation of his commission.

The Call to Sonship through Baptism

The New Testament reports of the baptism of Jesus at the beginning of his public ministry (Mark 1:9–13 par.) all contain references to a voice coming from heaven. This one voice testifies to Jesus as the beloved Son of God (cf. Luke 3:22). The original format is undoubtedly that of the mode of address adopted from Psalm 2:7: "You are my son, today have I begotten you." What does the use of the adoption formula for Jesus of Nazareth intend to express christologically? First, this: the baptism stories clearly recount the necessity that Jesus' consciousness of his commission must have indeed manifested itself in his biography. Of course, one quickly runs into an insurmountable limit, for the biblical text of Mark as well as of Luke do not provide an answer to *how* the consciousness of commission arose as it came to be expressed in Jesus' words and deeds and in his claim on authority, as well as in his readiness to suffer. It clearly has to do with the memory *that* this consciousness of commission had truly come about even though we have no direct knowledge of how it did so. We don't know *how*, but we know *that* it must have disclosed itself biographically in the life of Jesus. (This *that* is important inasmuch as it demonstrates that Jesus Christ was not some object without a will who was simply used by God or utilized, but rather a human being who, being capable of responding, was called into service and allowed himself to be called into it. In light of this, it may perhaps also become clear why prayer played such an important role for Jesus [cf. Mark 1:35;

6:46; 14:32]). If upon closer scrutiny the basis for Jesus' sonship of God through an act of adoption proves itself to be insufficient, the baptism of Jesus still maintains its christological significance in that it expresses *that* his calling and identity had manifested themselves to the human being Jesus of Nazareth in the course of his life's history.

The Birth of the Son of God by the Virgin Mary according to Matthew 1 and Luke 1

Why it is correct to call Jesus the Son of God is to be discussed in the following. A son must somehow be born. Upon closer reflection, however, a host of problems emerge:

- If Jesus Christ is understood as the result of an act of human procreation through the work of the Holy Spirit, then it is appropriate to ask how the end product could be both a "true God" and a "true man." Do we then not rather have to do with a half-god, at least if one understands the human act of procreation as having been replaced by the work of the Holy Spirit?

- The Virgin birth—at least from today's perspective—could lead to the idea that human sexuality must be excluded in order to describe the divine and thus also sinless origin of Jesus. This would clearly be grist for the mill of all moral sexual ethics since the time of Augustine.

- Moreover, one may well ask today what kind of view of women is actually hidden behind this idea. A purely passive one? Merely "receptive"?

What is to be communicated by the Virgin Birth? First, obviously, the real presence of Jesus in the space and time of the New Testament: namely, the *that* of Jesus Christ, *that* he was conceived through the Holy Spirit and *that* he became truly human in a particular time and in a particular place. Perhaps it is not at testimony of a biological miracle; perhaps the statement "born of the Virgin Mary" incorporated into the creed is connected to a symbolism current in the days of early Christianity according to which the mystery in the person of Jesus encompasses and defines Jesus' whole human life:

Jesus Christ was destined at birth for his assignment. The symbolism of the Virgin Birth seeks to portray at one and the same time the uniqueness of Jesus' life and journey as a uniqueness that consists in his singular endowment with the Holy Spirit intended for him from birth.

The Preexistence of the Son of God in John 1

The idea of preexistence goes deeper than the idea of adoption. Indeed, one could consider it an intensification of the models to the extent that divine origin is understood from a linear salvation-historical perspective (which obviously presents a bad construct!) and is moved "forward" again and again: from the resurrection (Paul) and baptism (Mark), then to the birth (Luke/Matthew), and finally, to the "pre"-existence of Jesus of Nazareth. What is being said here? First, the idea of preexistence expresses the eternity of the person of Jesus Christ with God. It says that the Son of God has belonged to God from eternity. As Paul says in Galatians, "but when the time had fully come, God sent his Son" (4:4). *God* became flesh in the man Jesus of Nazareth (John 1:14). Furthermore: Jesus is not one of us. He *comes* to us. The Logos—God himself—*comes* to us. He does not change, but brings everything that he has, namely his being. And that is love. As the Creator of the world, God since eternity is the one who will bring about this world's salvation as it is made known in Jesus. Finally, the relationship of God to the world is expressed in the idea of the creation of the world through Jesus Christ. In many places in the Bible, Christ is spoken of as the mediator of creation: "This cosmic meaning of Christ opens for all of world history a kind of horizon of divine mercy. God comes with his being into the world. And this being is love. And it prompts the theological thesis that such mercy of God is also active and perceivable outside the direct area of influence of the Christian message."[13] Thus there are dimensions that go beyond the efficacy, as it is perhaps perceived in the church. There is thus from the very beginning something akin to a cosmic dimension of reconciliation.

---

13. Kühn, *Christologie*, 316.

As a result two things can be seen: on the one hand, the divine origin of Jesus is presented in the New Testament not in a single model but in several models. This is a first signal that Christology is always (or better: from the beginning) plural. On the other, I find within this plurality an unambiguous message: the message of the *that* of the divine origin of Jesus of Nazareth. No doubt, Jesus is witnessed to as one who has his origin in God ,which later on becomes important for the understanding of God's saving activity—since only God can save! If we accept what was said above, we have an initial indication that Jesus Christ had to be on the level of experience of God's saving presence truly human and truly divine in order to reconcile in time and to save in eternity. He must be thought of as a true human being in order to save *us*, and true God, in order to *save* us.

In the history of dogma of early Christianity, two of the four New Testament models reemerge in overstated forms—namely, in so-called *adoptionism,* on the one hand, and *Docetism,* on the other. In the former, Jesus Christ was more human than divine, and in the latter more God than human. The adoptionism model (emerging with Theodotus of Byzantium, named the Tanner, around 190) amplifies the Markan model to such an extent that the "divine" in Jesus Christ becomes no longer sufficiently clear: Through baptism Jesus has become a "new" Moses, and came to be called the "Son of God" in figurative language. One speaks also of the "adoptionist monarchy" because in this model the monarchy of the one God was protected over against heathen polytheism. However, this version is hard to reconcile with the Markan model, because it is not clear that God encounters us in Jesus. This idea, namely, to put Jesus as the God-being in the middle, plays a central role in Docetism: here the Johannine idea of preexistence is reinforced so much that it is not sufficiently clear whether or not Jesus actually became human: he was a "phantom human." In Docetic teaching, the coming of the son of God excludes that the redeemer was a true human being. The biblical statements about the humanity of Jesus—for example, that he was thirsty—rather indicate a "semblance" (*Schein, dokesis*) of thirst. (Behind the conception of Docetism is a fundamentally critical, Gnostic view of the world that can conceive of redemption only as a detachment from everything earthly and that cannot relate God and the world one to another in a positive way).[14]

Figures of Adoptionism	Figures of Docetism

Jesus (in baptism) is adopted as Son	Jesus was only seemingly a true human

Accepting the Challenge of the "Scholarship-Faith": Why the Scholarly Objection Is Itself Historical

What are we to say after looking at the objection and the problems underlying it? Does Christology have to do with historically untenable faith-questions, indeed, has it become a pure "object of faith" or a "fantasy" of religious fanatics? Does Christian theology threaten to lose any connection to modern consciousness, which is permeated by much of historical research and its scholarly, scientific image?

A Note of Encouragement

- Behind the historical-scholarly objection there lies a modern understanding of history. The word "historical" seems to mean the same thing as "true" or "correct" if one understands the historian's aim to be discovering "what really happened" (Ranke). As against that, "faith" appears to be equivalent to "uncertain" or "only believed." In light of the intellectual-historical conditions of post-modernity, this dualism of modernity is itself

---

14. Graphics by René Koch, Berlin.

already historical: Namely, the acquisition of knowledge from history is currently judged widely to be itself "constructed,"[15] and the naïve-modern idea that *history is also true* has since been left behind.

- One should therefore no longer fear this objection—other than the fathers of the life-of-Jesus research—above all for reasons of theology. It belongs to the essence of faith to believe without "crutches," for indeed the historical reality of Jesus cannot be a "crutch," since faith is based on trust in God in the form of turning to Jesus Christ in the hope of something better.[16] Even historically detailed search for Jesus of Nazareth will not add to or subtract from this trusting faith (*"fides"* as *"fiducia"*).[17] History can never be a "crutch" and replace trust in God (whom one cannot see). "And even if it were possible (which logically isn't the case) to 'prove' historically that Jesus Christ did not rise from the dead, it would only show that the resurrection of the crucified one by God cannot be apprehended as an historically describable and explainable event, and that Christian faith is something other than faith in certain historical facts."[18]

- If one assumes that the New Testament is more like a sermon than a "factual report"—should one not be encouraged and strengthened in knowing that this "preached Christ" could have such historical impact? "One of the most astonishing things about the New Testament is that it says much more about Jesus than he about himself."[19] And if there are critics[20] who

---

15. On the basic understanding of "constructivism," according to which (in its most radical form) all knowledge resembles a cognitive construct, see Watzlawick, *Wie wirklich ist die Wirklichkeit?*; Fischer, *Die Wirklichkeit des Konstruktivismus*; Moser, *Komplexe Konstruktionen*.

16. See the evangelical concept of faith of Härle, *Dogmatik*, 55–80.

17. See the discussion of forms of faith in the more comprehensive contribution by Wüstenberg, "Fides implicita 'revisited'—Versuch eines evangelischen Zugangs."

18. Dahlferth, "Volles Grab, leerer Glaube?" 379. There is no room here to go into other noteworthy differences between an actual event and that which is describable historically, as Karl Barth describes it.

19. Thus, Martin Hailer in D. Ritschl, *Grundkurs*, 98.

20. Hick, *The Myth of God Incarnate*.

think that faith in the incarnation is a later interpretation—"historically late" in the sense of "therefore less reliable"—then one can respond with the following: In our discussion of the four models on the divine origin of Jesus we saw that the New Testament does not only (and not primarily) speak of incarnation. But does this then mean that faith endeavors to extract the most original form from the Bible in order to declare everything that comes later on to be secondary? The historical argument always contains a hidden value judgment (the more original equals more reliable which equals better for faith). Suppose we were able discover the most original layer—something that exegetical experts doubt: Who could decree then that only this and no other layer contains something true (and important for faith)?

- To put it boldly: Would Buddhists be shaken in their faith convictions because they did not have precise knowledge of the "historical Buddha," or because someone showed them a "more reliable," "more original" layer in the history of tradition? This comparison, at its most pointed edge, leads to the question of whether a Buddhist would think it important at all *that* Buddha had lived.[21]

- The historical study of the New Testament, as it was done in the second half of the twentieth century and still is until now, helps protect the Christian faith against a biblical fundamentalism. The idea that there is one biblical view of Jesus together with one teaching that one can extrapolate directly from the Bible into the political sphere and to which we, in defiance of the supposedly "complicated" and "cerebral" academic theologies, could return to, is a construct. From its beginning, theology has existed only as theologies. In the same way, Christology does not exist in the singular.

---

21. Clearly, the comparison is lacking a decisive soteriological position. Contrary to Buddhism, the Christian understanding of salvation is also based in the true humanity of Jesus. It is not insignificant whether Christ lived or not. Compare on this point the important contribution of Theo Sundermeier, "Erlösung oder Versöhnung."

4

Christology in a World of Spiritual Searching

Is Christology Something Other than a Dead Letter and Cold Belief in Dogma?

In the quest for spiritual mooring, the teaching of Jesus as the Christ faces a hard task. Objections arise already within the theological discussion. In the face of the abundance of the post-Easter stories about Jesus, the development of early church dogma is said to be curiously abstract. Critics regard the notion that God and humanity have come together in Jesus Christ a purely intellectual exercise. The christological dogma of Jesus Christ as "true God and true human" is rational, indeed bloodless, seeing that we are dealing with "bare, negative definitions" (A. von Harnack). The verdict: Christology always has something to do with cold, "dogmatic" statements that must be believed, instead of calling people today to make a decision for God. The typical characteristic of dogma is that it is abstract and poor in content, lacking in emotion and spiritually void. And was the Chalcedonian Creed not merely a political compromise anyway that "didn't solve anything"?[1] Fundamentalist criticisms, such as those cited above, have among other things led to historical relativization. Some theology students also ask, what are we to do with a dogma that is more than one and a half millennia old? Repeat it merely for

1. Simonis, *Jesus Christus, wahrer Mensch und unser Herr.*

the sake of right doctrine? Does the "old" dogma provide answers anyway to questions that we ask today? Is the development of the christological dogma not rather an intellectual genuflection before Greek philosophy by Christian theology (R. Bultmann)?

Challenging Dogmatic Christology

The historicizing challenge of the early church's development of the christological dogma came to a climax in the life-of-Jesus research in the nineteenth century. Increasingly, the development of the dogmatic tradition was critiqued in favor of an allegedly direct "historical" access to Jesus of Nazareth. People wanted to know finally who this Jesus was himself and not what the creed, the church, or tradition "claimed" about him. However, instead of one, true, historical Jesus, the first wave of historical Jesus research revealed a variety of "Jesus images," which—as Albert Schweitzer showed—most likely reflected the biographies of their authors. This in some respects naïve, direct approach to the supposedly true, "historical" Jesus of Nazareth has enjoyed a renaissance during the twentieth century in certain circles. One recalls the glowing reception of Jesus in the 1960s and early 1970s, in which Jesus was revered as a pacifist, social reformer, or revolutionary, as a hippie, political liberator, or archetype of true love and humanity! Later, Jesus was described as an eschatological prophet (E. P. Sanders), an exorcist (Graham Twelftree), a "Galilean Chassid" (Geza Vermes), and even as a "rustic Jewish cynic" (John Dominic Crossan).

A further wave of challenges to christological dogma, which primarily relativized his divinity, took place in circles describing themselves as "spiritual" and which are currently very influential. These are people who understand themselves to be "religious," but without any firm religious affiliation. In these circles, Jesus is regarded as a teacher, specifically as a teacher of a higher morality. At the same time, all statements that make a claim to his divinity or supernaturalness are rebuffed in these circles; the emphasis is entirely on his moral message. As a result, the Sermon on the Mount becomes the core of Christian teaching, as it was with the pacifist Jesus of the 1960s. In short: Jesus is an example of a spiritually and morally better conduct of life. Part of this portrayal is the emergence—at least in American circles—of the picture of a good Jesus, like that found in Sunday schools. The conception of Jesus as a teacher worthy of admiration and as an exemplary human being can also be shared by those who do not see themselves as Christian at all. One thinks of Mahatma Ghandi, who never stopped being a pious Hindu, but claimed that his method of nonviolent resistance was inspired by Jesus. Accordingly, if one conceives of Jesus in this way, one can confidently ignore the results of historical scholarship. His teachings and his personal example can therefore be admired or imitated regardless of what historians have to say about the individual figure they refer to.

In light of such attempts of direct approach to the "moral" Jesus, historical-critical biblical scholarship has shown that the Jesus proclaimed in the New Testament was not primarily a teacher of moral wisdom. The writings of the Apostle Paul already amply demonstrate that Jesus' teaching itself plays little or no role at all. Pauline theology is highly interested in the Savior Jesus. As more recent research[2] shows, the moral teachings of Jesus themselves essentially corresponded to Jewish tradition. Hence, one may ask: Does the morality of the Sermon on the Mount not become somehow meaningless if one removes it from the context of Jesus' proclamation of the imminently coming kingdom of God and turning it into an "everyday ethic"? Doesn't its "morality" have an eschatological character that allows little room for guiding principles of behavior in ordinary life? In any case, one can safely say that, with the exception of some saints, no one can live according to the principles of the Sermon on the Mount, at least that one would not survive for very long if one tried.[3]

2. Recently, Theissen, *Verhalten und Erleben der ersten Christen.*

3. In this connection, Luther makes a distinction between the Christian as a private person who must suffer the injustice that is done to him without retaliation, and the Christian as the public person (in a broad sense, as mother or father, teacher, mayor, policeman, or soldier) who has the job of placing himself in front of his neighbor to protect him and to shield him from violence and harm wherever possible, and to fight evil. From the modern perspective, it can be argued from a critical standpoint that Luther has either gone too far or not far enough in his interpretation of the Sermon on the Mount in formulating an "everyday ethic" of the life of the Christian as private person. In the former sense, it can be asked whether he possibly has underestimated the meaning of the representation of justice where it has to do with individual rights. The basis for Luther's underestimation could, however, lie in the fact that he wanted

CHRISTOLOGY IN A WORLD OF SPIRITUAL SEARCHING

The third wave of challenging the ancient church's christology is once again connected with the name of Rudolf Bultmann. He claimed that the worldview of the New Testament was thoroughly mythological. Bultmann defined "mythological" as "the use of imagery to express the other worldly in terms of this world and the divine in terms of human life, the other side in terms of this side."[4] That is, divine activity is viewed in analogy to human, earthly activity, and God's might and activity are discerned within the unexplainable events of history and nature. "The causality of the hereafter is incorporated into the chain of events of the world. . . . Myths speak of gods and of men [sic], of the deeds of gods as well as of human actions, except that the gods have super-human powers and their activities are irrational and capable of disrupting and destroying the natural course of things."[5] Therefore, the super-natural is superior to the natural. God's other-worldliness was accordingly conceived of as spatial distance which is why the ancient worldview is closely tied to mythology: The world is perceived of in three stories; the earth lies between heaven and the underworld; both divine and demonic powers made the earth a theater for their activities.

According to Bultmann, this world view is unacceptable for modern consciousness. If the Christian message is to be understood by modern women and men, then this mythological packaging must be unpacked. The language to be used for this so-called project of demythologizing was chosen by Bultmann from existential philosophy, particularly from Heidegger. From this philosophical basis, human existence can be comprehended as being alienated from its

---

to retain the strict linguistic antithesis of the Sermon on the Mount; but this argument against Luther is not aimed at the distinction between the private person and the professional person, but only against its use in relationship to oneself and to one's neighbor. In the latter sense, it can be asked whether Luther perhaps didn't go far enough when he "limited" the meaning of the Sermon on the Mount to the "area" of the private person "and underestimated the extraordinariness of the Christian life" (Bonhoeffer) to which the Beatitudes frees them (following DBW 4:57ff.). Compare here Szentpétery, "Ist die 'Nachfolge' eine radikale Kritik des Luthertums?" 155–66.

4. Bultmann, "The New Testament and Mythology," in Bartsch, *Kerygma and Myth*, 1:10 n. 2.

5. Bultmann, "Zum Problem der Entmytholosierung," in Bartsch, *Kerygma und Mythos*, 2:184.

true essence. The *kerygma* (Greek for "preaching," thus, the preaching of Jesus as the Christ) proclaims the freedom from alienation of the person from him or herself and from God. Bultmann interprets traditional Christian symbols with a new meaning that unties them from the supernatural thinking of the New Testament. It was thought that this project offered the Protestant church a better chance of survival in the modern world.

Clearly, Bultmann's project was very different from the moralism of liberal theology and, in addition, offered protection from the anxieties caused by historical scholarship. For the Christian faith now appears to be independent from the vicissitudes of historical research: not the historical Jesus, but rather the preached Christ is the starting point for faith. Bultmann insisted that Paul (and also John) were not interested in the teachings of Jesus himself nor, for that matter, in the historical Jesus. Rather, they focused entirely on the event that, for Paul, was revealed solely in the resurrection. Simply stated, for Bultmann it is thus:[6] during Jesus' time God was seen as present in Jesus. The early Christian community worshiped Jesus as a "divine" figure, "but not simply as God," as Bultmann emphasizes. Rather, Jesus was distinguished from God the Father. And none of the titles that Jesus was given—namely, "Son of God," "Son of Man"—had any reference to his nature (*physis*). They all are in reference to his revelation of God's word that is addressed to us. Bultmann is concerned neither with the historical Jesus nor with the dogmatic Christ, but with Jesus Christ present in the *kerygma*—the Christ *pro me*: "In this sense one may therefore say that in him God meets (us). The formula 'Christ is God' is false in the sense in which God is understood as an objectifiable entity, irrespective of whether it is understood in an Arian or Nicene, an Orthodox or Liberal sense. The formula is correct if 'God' is understood here as the event of God's action. But my question is, should one then not try to avoid such formulae on account of potential misunderstandings and confidently content oneself with saying that he is the Word of God?"

Later christological formulations, beginning with the Council of Nicea (325 CE) were, according to Bultmann, motivated by the

---

6. Following citations taken from Bultmann, "Das christologische Bekenntnis des Ökumenischen Rates," 155, 287.

necessity to express the Christian faith in the language of Hellenism, and on account of that he considers them no longer binding.

Even if one concedes that Bultmann's arguments are elegant and are indeed similar to an intellectual exercise that seems to sweep away the problems of modern historical research, one must at least take note of how calmly he puts all the agonizing christological debates of the early church, that we will presently discuss, behind him. And then there is the question of the validity of Bultmann's analysis of a "demythologized world," as well as the theological question of whether an existential interpretation is not too narrowly considered in view of the cosmic dimension of the reconciling activity of God in Jesus Christ.

In my opinion, sociologist of religion Peter L. Berger[7] correctly criticizes Bultmann's concept on two points: his conception of the modern consciousness is too narrow and that of mythology too broad. In his seminal lecture on demythologization,[8] Bultmann says that people who today use electric lights and radios, take advantage when they are sick of modern medicine and clinics, cannot accept the miracles and the mythological worldview of the New Testament. The sociologist Berger responds by saying that

> this is not a theological, but a *sociological* statement— and there is very little empirical evidence for it. The sociologist of contemporary religion can show that, with the exception of rather limited groups (prominent among them people with higher education in the humanities and social sciences), modern people are very capable indeed of accepting all sorts of miracles and full-blown "mythological" worldviews. Put simply, mythology is alive and well in the modern world. But Bultmann's view of mythology itself is too broad. It encompasses just about everything that most people have understood as religion. Curiously, as some of Bultmann's critics have pointed out, it *excludes* what he calls the "event" of God's presence in Jesus and in the kerygma. Should not this also be called "mythological"? If so, then nothing remains of

7. Berger, *Questions of Faith*, 73f.
8. Bultmann, "New Testament and Mythology," in *Kerygma and Myth*, 1:16–21.

Christianity beyond a somewhat eccentric philosophical understanding of the alienation or inauthenticity of the human condition, liberation from which could (and has been) just as well expressed in non-Christian language.[9]

However, I think there is something very important in Bultmann's argument, namely, that faith cannot be built on historical reconstruction of any sort. My faith in Christ can be based only in the recognition of the Christ for me, in the *kerygma*, as Bultmann would say. There is much to support the idea that one indeed encounters Christ in the *kerygma* of the proclaimed message. But this encounter finds meaning only if I can find the nexus between me and my own experience of reality; and this nexus cannot exclude the dogmatic aspects that Bultmann likes to call mythology.

The Unhappy Question of the "Natures" and the "Person" of Jesus, or, Jesus Was God and Human, but Other than We Think

Rudolf Bultmann rejected the so-called doctrine of the two natures for two reasons: first and foremost the philosophical modification of the portrayal of Jesus, and secondly and more subtly, dogmatic Christology may not have been kerygmatic enough for him; it does not meet the human existence that is called by the preached word of God into a decision. This objection points to a central problem of early church theology, namely, that it answers questions that are possibly no longer being asked that way today.

Next to the doctrine of the Trinity, Christology was the second greatest theological achievement of the ancient church, especially of the Eastern church. But what can one do today with these large doctrinal structures? It is highly questionable, linguistically (and theologically), whether one and the same concept "nature" should have been used synonymously for both the divine and the human at all. How are we to manage the conceptual transfer—from the Greek thought and conceptual world of the first three centuries, to

---

9. Berger, *Questions of Faith*, 61.

an understanding of nature and person in the twenty-first century? Does Christology have any way answer questions we ask today?

The decision presented by ancient church christology at the fourth ecumenical council of Chalcedon (451) was a highly balanced, differentiated, intellectual response to questions that had spell-bound the young church since the first centuries. How can God be present in the human being Jesus? During this period, unstable and erroneous positions—such as the versions of adoptionism and Docetism—were rejected. But does the "doctrine of the two natures" also provide answers to questions believers ask *today*? The first thing to be noted is that there is no direct answer to a central question that Dietrich Bonhoeffer had formulated in unsurpassed simplicity in his prison cell in Tegel: "Who is Christ actually for us today?"[10] There is much to be said for the fact that the issue today is no longer primarily the philosophical question: How is Jesus to be conceptualized? How is what I know to be ordered? And obviously it is also no longer a question of knowledge: Is that about Jesus really true historically? Not does it have to do with the classical examination question about the *what* of the council's decisions ("one person in two natures"). The "who question"[11] focuses on something facing us (*ein Gegenüber*) as an unknown, as if it were something that could actually tell me something new that I myself cannot tell myself or find out on my own. This *Gegenüber* can neither be coordinated with nor classified readily into everything known to me and at my disposal. Who is this Jesus? Whoever asks this question is bound to hear something amazing or strange.

First, there is this: Jesus, about whom we will learn that he is truly human and truly God, was different—different than every one of our images of him, whether before, during, or after the historical Jesus research. Already, the interpretations of his divine origin indicate this! For the following section it is decisive that we keep the

10. Bonhoeffer, *Letters and Papers from Prison*, 362. On this, cf. the classification of Bonhoeffer's prison theology in Plant, *Bonhoeffer*, 94–97.

11. Bonhoeffer's "who question" connects his prison theology with his lectures on Christology of 1933, in which the guiding question is that of the mystery of the person. See Bonhoeffer, *Berlin, 1932–1933*, 302. On the Christology of Bonhoeffer, see the recent work by Daub, *Die Stellvertretung Jesu Christi*, 486ff.

fullness of the biblical background in mind, since it is not always retained in this plurality in sketches of the early church's development. Whatever is clarified in dogma in terms of concepts must continually be explained anew from the multiplicity of biblical narratives. The Jesus whom dogma presents can only be the Jesus as the Scriptures present him. Biblically and dogmatically it is about the reason for Jesus' coming (for his "mission"), about the connection between Jews and heathen that was created by the Jew Jesus, about the justification and sanctification of the faithful, as well as about the future of humanity and of the world. "The question, who is Jesus Christ for us today? can only be appropriately treated in listening to the entire biblical witness and within the conceptual framework of the doctrine of the Trinity; that is, in an effort to understand the interlinking of Israel's election, God's participation in the suffering and death of humans, and God's healing activity in the Spirit."[12]

Jesus was different. His was a divine origin! With respect to his humanity, can we not count at least on some correspondences here? Unfortunately, we cannot. Let's just take the simple but very real experience no one is spared from: there basically seems to be no human being who can love. A human being who loves makes God's love real only approximately; his or her love is in a certain way a resplendence of the love of God. A human who can love is thus ultimately not one of the possibilities open to humankind: neither the ultimate aim of social developments nor the archetype of what it is to be human, nor the great promise that slumbers unborn somewhere in human history. The human being who can love is to be found fully realized only in the figure of Jesus of Nazareth, in the being of the "new" human. This means first of all that this new human being of love stands as an indictment against everything that is otherwise called being human. One can ask about him only in astonishment: Who are you? For what his love represents, and how little a human possibility that one could simply implement, is captured by Paul in the unforgettable words, "Love is patient; love is kind; love is not envious or boastful or arrogant or rude. It does not insist on its own way; it is not irritable or resentful; it does not rejoice in wrongdoing, but rejoices in the

---

12. D. Ritschl, *Grundkurs*, 129.

truth. It bears all things, believes all things, hopes all things, endures all things" (1 Cor 13:4–7 NRSV).

Jesus embodies this love; indeed, he *was* this human being, and precisely in that he was other than how we can ever be. He was a human being of flesh and blood as we are and yet was entirely other than humans ordinarily are.[13] Metaphorically speaking, Jesus manifested "the divine measure of all humanity" and revealed the "humanity of God."[14] In other words: Jesus was human in a manner not known otherwise of humans. He showed the humanity, that is God's philanthropy, that encourages human beings to be human and nothing but human.

Jesus is one of us—indeed, he is our brother; many repeat this perception: Jewish thinkers such as Martin Buber, and also Hindus such as Mahatma Gandhi; and yet Jesus was—already in this!—other, someone higher, our Lord. Recently, such things are spoken less openly. Why? Because it is offensive, even irritating? Brother yes, Lord, no?

Who is this Jesus (Matt 16:18)? This mystery of this person is what the confession of the Christian faith seeks to address, from its post-Easter beginnings to the formulation of the so-called doctrine of the two natures, and beyond it to the time of the Reformation and in the questions concerning the Lord's Supper, right up to the present time. In the process, the line of development, characterized by the labors of conceptualizing the substance of faith, leads into ever new interpretive approaches to the classical dogma of Christ that had been formulated with the ontological means that Greek metaphysics had sought understanding.

Before we go any further, we note that the ancient church's doctrine has the advantage over against the life-of-Jesus research in that focusing on Jesus being different allowed the question "Who is Jesus?" to be raised at all. The ancient church's christology searched for an answer to the first part of that same question Bonhoeffer was to raise later. For the hermeneutical second part of his question—*for*

---

13. The formulation of the christological dogma makes reference to this when it says "and is like us in our humanity [*homoousios*] in every way except sin."

14. Stauffer, *Jesus war ganz anders*, 8f.

us today?—ancient christology set framing conditions above all, as we shall see later, in relation to "what just won't do."

A "Non-solution" as Solution: Jesus Christ Is Utterly beyond Conceptualization

Who was this Jesus Christ? How is the presence of God in the human being Jesus to be conceived? How does the eternal Godhead in this one person Jesus Christ relate to that person's true humanity? How can the one person of Jesus Christ be conceived of as a unity when in him two contrasting natures of origin are to be distinguished?

"True God": Is the "God in Jesus" the Same as the "God" of Israel? Preliminaries Set in the Doctrine of the Trinity

Preceding the christological "how" question with respect to the divine and human natures of the person of Jesus Christ, there is the third- and fourth-century question of the Trinity: how does the assumed divinity of Jesus Christ relate to the (not exclusively Jewish) demand of monotheism? Do we encounter in Jesus a "second" God? Is the "God in Jesus" the same as the "God" of Israel? The controversies of the third and fourth centuries, fought frequently over "Aryan" or "Trinitarian" struggles, cannot be even approximately outlined here.[15] A preliminary settlement of the controversy was adopted in 325 CE at the First Ecumenical Council of Nicea. There, a dogmatic formula was formulated: Jesus is begotten and not created and is of one being with the Father (Greek *homoousios*). Its implementation addressed an underlying concern to make certain that by affirming the Godhead of Jesus Christ, the monotheism of the Jewish tradition would not be undermined. The divine in Jesus is entirely and completely the same eternal substance of the Father. The Son has no other being than that of the Father; he is in no way an adopted Son, but is entirely a "son of essence." In other words: the divinity of Jesus is always God himself. Speaking metaphorically: *in Jesus, God himself*

---

15. Compare the overview in Andresen, *Handbuch der Dogmen- und Theologiegeschichte*, 1:144–221.

appears. This has nothing to do with a remote working of the divine power of creation and reason (*logos*), but with the perfection of God's *logos* as this human being. *Logos* does not *have* a human being, the *logos is* human being. However, the acknowledgment of the divinity of Jesus overturns all subsequent language about God. For now it is the case that "I am with you now and to the end of the age" (Matt 28:20). Speaking of Christ being present to us this way is directly or indirectly tied to the insights of the doctrine of the Trinity (key word: *homoousios*). What is established here is that in *Jesus Christ* we are in *essence* dealing with *God*:

- with his presence in the Word and in the sacraments;
- with his presence in persecution, suffering, and martyrdom;
- with his presence in personal prayer and in mystical immersion;
- with the form and interpretation of our life and our entire situation from the perspective of God's presence.

"Truly Human": How Can God Be Present in a Human Being? Apollinaris of Laodicea

Whatever one wants to identify as deficits of the council's Christology, there is no doubt that the theologians whose position in matters christological prevailed during the first centuries sought to safeguard the true "humanity," the actual humanity of Jesus, under all circumstances. The fight against Docetism was carried out with determination, for the sake of the salvation of humankind, indeed, for the sake of the complete reconciling and saving activity of God. And so, Jesus Christ must also have been the same as we are, therefore *homoousios* with humans (only without sin), otherwise he could not have saved (sinful) humankind through his death and resurrection. It was as it were the basic assumption, indeed the basic premise, that God acts for our salvation in Jesus Christ and that Jesus brings "our humanity" to God. To believe this it only makes sense if Jesus was truly and without diminution human. The theological achievement of the later fourth and early fifth centuries consisted in bringing this thought to its ultimate conclusion: How can God be in Jesus? How can the eternal Son (the second person of the Trinity, the logos from eternity, *homoousios* with the eternal Father) be *in* Jesus, in a human being? How can the *"apathic"* God be connected to a *"pathic"* human being? This remained the unsolved question if one did not want to take the *docetic* view of God as only seemingly connected to the sufferings of earth-bound human reality.

Apollinaris, bishop of Laodicea, took this matter up with rigor. For him, it was clear from the beginning: Jesus must have been more and something other than a prophet inspired by God. Apollinaris developed his ideas on the basis of Greek anthropology that saw human beings as "consisting" of spirit, flesh, and soul. In this anthropological model, the flesh is fickle and needs to be guided by the mind (*nous*). Correspondingly, Apollinaris taught that the logos becoming flesh in Jesus Christ is to be interpreted thusly: the logos takes the place of the (human) spirit and connects itself with the (human) flesh that is regarded as inspired with a soul. The fickle flesh thus proceeds to its salvation under the firm guidance of the *logos*. In summary: *The human mind/spirit (nous) of Jesus is replaced by logos*. However, this means that Jesus could not have been fully and truly human, but only "partially" so. And that implies that only portions of the human can be "brought to God," that is, be saved. Now, if the logos assumes inspired flesh, what about human reason? What the logos has not assumed can therefore not be saved, said the great theologian Gregory of Nazianzus. One must connect the entire human being to the logos if the entire human being is to be saved. The *whole* divinity must be *wholly* with the humanity. *Becoming* human (incarnation) is interesting only insofar as in it human beings in "all their components" (flesh, body, and soul) are *assumed*. However, in order to explain this idea, other concepts were required.

From a hermeneutical perspective, the question still remains whether the emphasis on the actual humanity of Jesus in relation to humanity's salvation and redemption can be gleaned directly from the Gospels, or whether it does not lend credence to the idea that the central elements of classical christology—in its critical debate with, and as a counter-concept to, the religious groups and currents of the time (such as, among others, Gnosticism and Docetism)—were derived from a theoretical conception of salvation.[16] In any case, it is

---

16. On the contrast between redemption and reconciliation, see D. Ritschl, *Grundkurs*, 133f. Dietrich Bonhoeffer also classifies reconciliation at a higher

apparent that the soteriological idea dominated the period and to a great degree dominated the lines of argument. The idea of Jesus' unity of being with the Father led to the decision against any notion that humans are able to save themselves. God's reconciling and saving activity has priority over the ethical-religious demands of existence. In the sense of Bonhoeffer's "for us today" question, and in view of the ethical challenges, it must be asked whether we can with the same basis—namely the question of "being saved"—confirm the real humanity of Jesus, or whether there are possibly very different, new reasons for doing so.

Divine and Human "in One": The Alexandrian Tradition

Gregory of Nazianzus and the other two "great Cappadocians" (Basil the Great and Gregory of Nyssa) developed a doctrine in which, on the one hand, the logos of God and, on the other, the human being are viewed in terms of mind, body, and soul. Both supposedly came together in the birth by Mary in such a way that a "mixture" was created in which the divine permeated the human. The different natures were combine themselves as it were into a unity. The ideas of the Cappadocians are taken up and developed further in the so called *Alexandrian Tradition*. Its main representative was Cyril of Alexandria, who died in 444 CE. The question associated with that tradition was formed by the soteriological theme of redemption, which could be conceived of only through the incarnation and the close union of the divine and the human. The question was: how does the logos become flesh (*sarx*)? At first, the answer was: God must altogether become human so that we may be redeemed. And this complete *unity* of God and human in Jesus Christ is what is to be clarified and declared. Opponents subsequently described this approach as the doctrine of *the one* nature (monophysitism).

---

level than a "religion of redemption." He disputes that the "essence of the proclamation of Christ" is the redemption from "sorrows, hardships, anxieties, and longings, out of sin and death, in a better life beyond." Rather, since Christians do not seek "an ultimate escape route . . . into eternity" but—like Christ—drink "earthly life to the last drop," "the Crucified and Risen One" is with them completely, "and they are crucified and resurrected with Christ." Bonhoeffer, *Letters and Papers from Prison*, 447–48.

Divine and Human Must Be Held Apart: The Antiochenes

Another school of thought came together in Antioch. Its main representatives were Diodorus of Tarsus, who died shortly before 395 CE, Theodore of Mopsuestia, who died in 429 CE, and later on Nestorius, who died after 439 CE. The question associated with this tradition was not oriented primarily by the soteriological-dogmatic theme of redemption, but by a problem, namely: How can we make sense exegetically that the person Jesus is Logos/Christ? How can one, within the framework of the decisions of the Trinitarian dogma—namely, that in Jesus God encounters us (in the second person of the Trinity)—come to terms with what the New Testament tells us about Jesus? The answers to these questions, it is true, did have an impact on soteriology. The Antiochene School taught that the person of Jesus (with body, soul, and mind) of his own free will forged a way to unity with the logos of God. From the beginning, the logos joins himself to this process through the mediation of the spirit. The connection between both becomes progressively closer and leads after Jesus' death to a complete unity of action, power, honor, and veneration. The unity of the two natures of Jesus and the logos cannot be conceived of as a natural interpenetration, for this assumption implies a blending which erases the uniqueness of both Jesus and the logos. But it can be understood in terms of the categories of action and relationship: In parallel action the two come together into one "role" (Greek: *prosopon*) and in this "role" the person of Jesus is given the honor due to the logos. Theodore of Mopsuestia,[17] who was arguably the most important representative of the Antiochene School, formulated it this way: the logos perfects the human being Jesus "in the union with him into a single *prosopon* and bestowed on him a share in the fullness of power; and so he effects all in him and so that through him and his parousia he also perfects the judgment the world."

---

17. Cited in Karpp, *Textbuch zur altkirchlichen Christologie, Theologia und Okonomia*, 109.

Solution via a Conceptual Non-solution: The "Christological Controversy" and the So-Called Doctrine of the Two Natures of Chalcedon

It was obvious that there was going to be a conflict about how the two proposals presented the togetherness of the logos of God and the human conceptually. It started as a controversy over Mary in the year 428 CE, when the Antiochene monk and scholar Nestorius became patriarch of Constantinople. There he encountered a popular piety that venerated Mary as the one who gave birth to God as the mother of God. In a sermon, Nestorius takes a critical stance: We cannot and must not call Mary the mother of God, but one ought to speak of her as the "bearer of Christ." Behind this statement is the Antiochene tradition that Nestorius had embraced: In Jesus Christ the divine and the human are to be clearly distinguished, albeit not to be separated, for, as he says: "We indeed don't have two Christs and not two sons, for one and the same is a duality, not in rank, but in nature."[18] Nestorius seeks to present the unity of this duality (as we saw earlier Theodore of Mopsuestia did too), in the Greek concept of *prosopon*: "The *prosopon*, the companion of the two natures, is Christ."[19] According to this understanding of Jesus Christ, Mary could not have given birth to the preexisting logos, could not be the mother of God. But, conversely, she would also not be the mother of an ordinary human being, that is to say bearer of a human being; rather she bore the human being to whom the logos of God is related from eternity and who himself is related to the logos—indeed, this being-in-relation-to is to be conceived of in such a way that one can no longer separate either in the subject of Christ. If the unity of this relation is to be spoken of as Christ, then Mary should be called "the bearer of Christ."

Cyril, patriarch of Alexandria, disagreed. He said that for the sake of our salvation, Mary must be called mother of God and bearer of God. In accepting the statements of the Cappadocians and the Alexandrian school, he argued that if God's logos actually joined himself with human reality then it must already be present in Mary's womb, so that Mary together with the human, reason-instilled flesh gave birth to the logos of God. "The logos has become human and

18. Ibid., 116.
19. Ibid., 118.

has been named the Son of Man, because in an inarticulable and inconceivable way united himself with flesh instilled with a reason-inspired soul."[20] Cyrill goes so far as to say that, after the incarnation, the differences being fully acknowledged, one can speak really only of *one* incarnated nature of the Son.

This controversy was unavoidable and continued, at times with more, at others with less furor, for over two centuries. All sorts of unpleasant side effects also emerged with it: political ambition of patriarchs, interventions of the imperial court and the emperor, distortions, slander, intrigues, and the billy clubs of stirred up mobs of monks. What was it all about? *How is the preexistent Son of God to be thought of and conceptualized as being together with the human being of Jesus?* Two competing interests stood opposite one another: One, for the sake of our salvation, seeks to connect the human being Jesus with the preexistence of the Son of God as closely as possible: God is near to us in Jesus (Apollinaris, the Cappadocians, Cyril, Eutyches). The others are moved to discern and to present the preexisting logos and the human being in their uniqueness. Both arguments are critical of the other. From the point of view of the Alexandrians, the Antiochenes divide Jesus Christ into a God and a man, and are incapable of showing their unity. And that cheats us human beings of our salvation. From the point of view of the Antiochene camp, the Alexandrians commix the human being of Jesus so much with the logos of God that he becomes a divine mongrel and thus no longer a truly human being. And so, we human beings are likewise cheated of our salvation. Clearly, both arguments tend to be ambiguous. One can interpret the Alexandrian position excessively in terms of the commixture of God and the human so that one overlooks the clear attempt of Cyril to distinguish the two natures. Similarly, one can look at the Antiochene position as one that separates the Son of God and the Son of Man, even as one overlooks Nestorius' very clear attempt to combine them through his broad interpretation of the category of *prosopon* in relation also to the two natures.[21]

---

20. Ibid., 120.
21. Graphics by René Koch, Berlin.

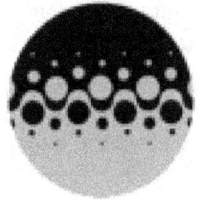 

MIXED   SEPARATED

Both Alexandrians and Antiochenes seek to hold the preexisting logos, on the one hand, and the human being Jesus, on the other, together conceptually. Both tend to speak of the incarnate logos as of one person and two natures. But while the Alexandrians seem to speak not only of *one person* but also of *one nature* of Jesus Christ, the Antiochenes in contrast seem to speak not only of *two natures* but also of *two persons*. The confusion is only compounded by the category of the *person* for which the Antiochenes use the Greek word *prosopon*, whereas the Alexandrians inceasingly use the Greek word *hypostasis*.[22] Is Christology then just a labyrinth, a maze of concepts? How does one make one's way?

The Council of Chalcedon (451 CE) tried to clarify the Christology conflict. Its decision confirmed the Trinitarian confession of Nicea. It incorporated relevant statements from a treatise Pope Leo I had sent to the patriarch of Constantinople, made reference to statements by Cyril as well as to a joint text the patriarchs John of Antioch and Cyril of Alexandria had composed in 433 CE. The influence of the emperor made itself felt here as it had in Nicea. The process resulted in the following declaration:

> We, then, following the holy Fathers, all with one consent, teach people to confess one and the same Son, our Lord Jesus Christ, the same perfect in Godhead and also perfect in manhood, truly God and truly human, of a reasonable soul and body; consubstantial [*homoousios*] with

---

22. D. Ritschl (*Grundkurs*, 116) makes a graphic, albeit highly simplified suggestion, that the Greek concept of *hypostasis*, for which there is neither a Latin nor a German equivalent, "be compared to the branches of a firm that has no 'headquarters,' but that is fully represented by and present in its three hypostases, each of which has different tasks to fulfill."

CHRISTOLOGY

the Father according to the Godhead, and consubstantial [*homoousios*] with us according to the Manhood; in all things like unto us, without sin; begotten before all ages of the Father according to the Godhead, and in these latter days, for us and for our salvation, born of the Virgin Mary, the Mother of God, according to the Manhood; one and the same Christ, Son, Lord, only-begotten, to be acknowledged in two natures, inconfusedly, unchangeably, indivisibly, inseparably; the distinction of natures being by no means taken away by the union, but rather the property of each nature being preserved, and concurring in one Person [*prosopon*] and one Subsistence [*hypostasis*], not parted or divided into two persons, but one and the same Son, and only-begotten God, the Word, the Lord Jesus Christ; as the prophets from the beginning have declared concerning Him, and the Lord Jesus Christ Himself has taught us, and the Creed of the holy Fathers has handed down to us.[23]

This then is what the solution means: the one Christ, who is wholly God and wholly human, must be thought of as *one* (being) in *two natures*. Both natures are united in one person—that is, *hypostasis*—and they are so:

- inconfusedly and unchangeably (contra Eutyches~Alexandria);
- indivisibly and inseparably (contra Nestorius~Antioch).

Did these four negative formulations (according to what in Greek grammar is called an alpha-privative) provide the solution? Can intellectual theology express the mystery of God's presence only in negative terms, that is, can it only say what it is *not*?

Two Attempts at an Understanding

The surprising thing about this decision is initially that no christological design as such is formulated for there is manifestly no intention

---

23. English translation is from N. S. Gill, "The Chalcedonian Creed." Online: http://ancienthistory.about.com/od/monotheisticreligions/g/chalcedon-creed.htm.

to provide a solution to the christological question with regard to content; on the contrary, the question is to remain open. The aim is to establish guidelines that any christological theory simply has to take into consideration. And what is determinative is not what the dogma makes possible in terms of content, but rather what it rejects. Any and all obvious simplifications are rejected that would comprise a rationalization of the portrayal of Jesus. Thus, Jesus Christ is not to be thought of as one who proceeds from two essences (the divine and the human) and then to exist in one of them. Nor is he to be thought of as one who from the outset consists of two essences so that a unity proceeds from them. In both theories it is not the God-human unity of person of Jesus Christ as such that is being debated—that is, not the actuality of the incarnation. What is at issue is how there can be a God-human unity at all, that is, the possibility of incarnation. In response to the question of the *how* of the incarnation, the christological dogma responds with two double negatives, namely, by declaring that this is precisely the question that cannot be asked meaningfully. We are left with Bonhoeffer's "who question" and the concern to protect the incarnation: "The Chalcedonian formula is an objective, living assertion about Christ that goes beyond all conceptual forms. Everything is encompassed in its very clear yet paradoxical agility."[24]

What becomes evident in the first place is why at this juncture the dogma could go no further than these negations. Jesus Christ is in no way amenable to conceptual deduction. He remains one removed from our grasp—an irritant to the Jews, and folly to the Greeks (1 Cor 1:23). The dogma is only true in that it makes room for the future of Jesus announced in Holy Scripture and thereby places itself back into the tentativeness of time. It cannot either be detached from the narrative linguistic connections of the Bible or seek conceptually to surpass it. Dogma is formed from the narrative language of the biblical canon and the concepts themselves are only valid within their own biblical contentiousness. In other words: the open and not closed biblical canon depicts the free space of Jesus Christ that the four negations of the christological dogma circumscribe. And all further reflection about the confession of Christ is to take place in this space. For example, we must consider that in

---

24. Bonhoeffer, *Berlin, 1932–1933*, 343.

Jesus Christ we are dealing with an actual human being. That fact was continually obscured in the course of the first centuries, right up to the monophysitism that Chalcedon rejected once and for all. As Ulrich Kühn says,

> It is a human being with a human history in whom God reveals himself and turns to us and the world: that is the actual message of Chalcedon over against Nicea. Christians do not believe and proclaim a myth, but the message of a human being, of his astonishing proclamation, his weakness, his struggle for God's will and his suffering. Chalcedon affirms christologically what is especially important for us today and what is given attention also beyond the boundaries of the church. We are dealing with someone who fascinates, who is credible in his alternative message and way of life, and who offers an important life task for the way into the future. There, in this human history and person—and not in a half-divine being or in a myth—God encounters us.[25]

Secondly, in reference to the Chalcedonian decision, we must consider the central concept of both natures (*physis*) "in Jesus Christ." Does it arise from an ontology of nature that simply does not do justice to the categories actually appropriate to personal history? We have already referred to the meaning of the concept of nature Chalcedon used in the light of such a critical question.

Bonhoeffer rejected the thesis of his teacher Adolf von Harnack that the Chalcedonian definition was the result of the Hellenization of Christianity and notes, "Liberal theologians say that it was the introduction of the concept of nature that has corrupted all of dogma. But it must be said in opposition that nothing is further from being a product of Greek thinking than the Chalcedonian formula."[26] In fact, the formulation of the "one person" and the "two natures" is relatively absurd for Greek philosophy, because in Hellenistic thinking the person participates only as one nature.

If the basic underlying concepts of nature are to be understood neither from the ancient Greek world nor in light of the modern

---

25. Kühn, *Christologie*, 160.
26. Bonhoeffer, *Berlin, 1932–1933*, 352.

concept of the physical, what then can be said that is theologically meaningful about the rather unfortunate talk of the difference of the two natures? I mean this: Jesus has a human consciousness, with questions, and the possibility of growth and maturation, but only because he is one with the Father. And precisely because (not: although) Jesus knows himself to be fully at one with the Father does he have an entirely human consciousness. In the unity, divinity and humanity are really together (indivisibly), but only so that both may appear in their full uniqueness (inconfusedly) because God is only then true God when he is with the human and the human being is only then truly human, when he is with God. According to Johannes Wirsching,

> Thus, the difference of natures is logically to be understood not as additional, but as proportional; [the difference] is not conveyed by the unity of the person to itself, but actually heightened in order to demonstrate this unity. All differences serve the unity, but this unity is not possible without differentiation. The closer the unity, the more apparent the differences! The Chalceonian definition differentiates in order to unify and unifies in order to differentiate. This means concretely: the more unambiguously Jesus is divine, the more unambiguously he is human. The more clearly I recognize God in Jesus, the more clearly I recognize him as intrinsically human.[27]

Such a proportional relationship is, in its core, also a relationship of agreement and of substantiation; a relationship of mutuality and not one of opposition. It is not: the more Jesus is human, the less he is God, and vice versa. In a proportional relationship, any one thing corresponds in that it corresponds to the other and also to itself. Through the fulfillment of the one the other is fulfilled. In the unity with the other, one grasps unity with oneself and vice versa. Choosing oneself at the same time means choosing the other and in the other's freedom one gains one's own. Once again Wirsching: "If therefore the presence of God in Jesus is thought of proportionally, then it will be thought of holistically and in the schematic of mutual support: the closer God is to the human being Jesus, the closer this

---

27. Wirsching, "Menschwerdung," 433.

human being is to himself. And, in the obverse, the more the human being Jesus wills that God is God, the more he can will that he himself is human (and not a half-god). The more effectual God's power, the more real the human being's authority! The clearer God's image, the more unambiguous God's likeness!"[28] In Jesus Christ, the original image shines through; we look into the Father's heart, as Luther says in the Catechism. The idea of proportionality reflects in its core the inner relationship between God and human, which after the fall (*post lapsum*) is experienced and thought of not as unity but as separation: either God *or* human; the *more man*, thus *less God* (and vice versa). In Jesus Christ this separation—or anti-proportionality—is overcome.

Accepting the Challenge of "Spiritualism": Why the Doctrine of the Two Natures Does Not Represent a Cold Dogmatic Belief but Remains Important as a "Regulator"

What is to be said in conclusion about the Chalcedonian definition? Are its defenders right in the end? Or its critics? Does it have to do with an intellectual exercise, with a "cold" dogma, a "cold, negative determination" as Harnack put it? Or is the dogma a "guardian of the mystery surrounding the person of Jesus Christ" (Wirsching)? Is it merely a political "compromise" (Simonis), indeed a genuflection on the part of Christian theology before Greek philosophy, and thus no longer binding (Bultmann)? Or is this dogma at least useful as an "intellectual toolbox" or some kind of theological "diagnostic device" to identify false statements about Jesus Christ (D. Ritschl)?

A Note of Encouragement

Even if one brands the dogma and its development as an intellectual exercise—what is wrong with that? To engage the person of Jesus with the mind must not *per se* be something evil. Is it not an aspect of intellectual integrity to be accountable for one's convictions? And at the heart of the convictions of Christian theology stands the person of Jesus Christ. To give an account for what one believes should

28. Ibid., 435.

moreover be a rule for Christian theology, just as it should be for the other religions or nonreligious convictions and worldviews. And does the insight, gained through the engagement of our intellect, that Jesus Christ was truly divine and truly human (and not a half-god upon which to put our trust) not protect us from every form of divinizing demigods fashioned by humans and from venerating idols—whether then or now?

Furthermore, it is easy to admit that over against the fullness of New Testament statements about Jesus Christ, the Chaldceondian definition seems abundantly abstract and stinting in its statements, seeing that in an analytical sense the definition is a formulation of a "regulative statement" (D. Ritschl). Whatever is clarified in the dogma conceptually must always be interpreted anew out of and from the multiplicity of the biblical testimony. Can the function of a dogma in fact not be illustrated on the basis of the Chalcedonian definiton?[29] The Council's decision establishes what false theology is. Can this not be viewed as an advantage? One needs to think only of the prodigious post-Easter language-gain in the Bible and the linguistic and pictorial traditions of postbiblical times: no shortage here, but overabundance. In times of a multiplicity of voices speaking of Jesus Christ, it is good to have instruments by which to orient oneself; or even to have regulative statements at the ready. In such situations of diverse Christian religious representation, it is the first function of dogma to test, to distinguish, and to provide orientation. Wherever this occurs in the sense of a "diagnostic device" it is completely appropriate!

Let us take this idea a bit further: dogma must necessarily be abstract and low on content if it is to fulfill the named functions. Dogmas are like tools: they regulate and test but do not replace that which they regulate, namely the content of the biblical and post-biblical fullness of proclamation, didactic language, and metaphor. The Chalcedonian definition expresses in unparalleled clarity the "true humanity" of Jesus in a regulative sense. Without the "intellectual, christological conflict" and the dogma of Chalcedon, the true humanity of Jesus would not have been formulated and established as authoritatively. In the human being Jesus Christ, God truly meets

---

29. On the following, see M. Hailer in D. Ritschl, *Grundkurs*, 140.

us. All modern and post-modern spirituality is ultimately grounded in this thought.

And finally, we must concede that the Chalceonian definition is a "compromise" in that it looked for the smallest common denominator between the Alexandrian and the Antiochene schools. But are both of these directions really historical, or is it not rather the case that in them—as the times of the Reformation have shown—they compress the continually present possibility of Christology into formulae so that the compromise has great potential?

But there are reasons why one may rightfully challenge the view that the great theological achievements of the fourth and fifth centuries in the doctrines of the Trinity and Christology are a genuflection of theology before Greek philosophy, which ultimately amounts to a falsification of the real issue. On the basis of linguistics alone, both of these great theological proposals are relatively absurd for Greek philosophical thought—and admittedly so! But in the very absurdity of their formulations, the Christian dogmas retain something very important: their language about God is always such "that it delves into the dimension of the mystery. We are able to speak of God, because it pleases God to make himself known in his chosen people, in his Son, through his spirit."[30] Consciously paradoxical dogmatic formulations clearly make the point that speculative thinking about God is of no help, but rather leads astray. There always remains something more, something beyond the grasp of reason, something that seeks to enter the heart. Once more Bonhoeffer: "The early church Christology really originated at the cradle of Bethlehem, and the splendor of Christmas lies on its eroded countenance. Even today, this Christology wins the hearts of those who come to know it."[31]

---

30. D. Ritschl, *Grundkurs*, 141.
31. Bonhoeffer, "Meditation on Christmas, December 1939," 529–30.

5

Christology in a World of Humanism and Human Rights

How Can a Loving God Stage the Death of His Son in Such a Gruesome Drama?

Since the time of humanism and the Enlightenment, arguments against the idea that Jesus Christ died "for us" and especially "for our sins" have been quite dominant. These arguments have been particularly leveled against the "for us"—namely, the idea of vicarious representation, as well as the concept of God that exists behind the *"died 'for us.'"* The claim is that human being's guilt and sin are not capable of being represented, but that they rather belong to the indispensable worth of the person (Kant). In view of this, it is neither intellectually comprehensible nor ethically responsible to think of sin and guilt in such a way that someone else could vicariously take them upon him or herself. Must acknowledgment and processing of guilt, repentance, and change—if they are to be effective—not take place within ourselves? What kind of picture of God hides behind such assumptions? Why must a sinless person die on the cross in such a horrifying way so that people can be in right relationship with God again? Why was the expiatory sacrifice of Jesus Christ necessary to reconcile humans with God? Is God not cruel to allow an innocent person to suffer? Is God not love? Could he not simply have erased the guilt of humanity in one magnificent act of forgiveness (a question first asked by Abelard)?

The Enigma of the Person of Jesus Christ and the Question of His Acts "For Us"

In the Christology of the ancient church, both traditional schools of thought were guided by a *paradigm of understanding*: The Antiochenes asked, how do the statements of the New Testament fit in with the doctrines of the Trinity? Must the natures, especially human nature, not have a certain degree of autonomy so that justice is done to the New Testament's statements? Or was one guided by the *paradigm of redemption*: The Alexandrians asked, how can I be redeemed? How do I explain that Christ became *sarx*? For any Christian at that time, just as today, the redemption warranted through Christ was present openly: in the worship service, in the reading of the Gospel, in the Eucharist. And these events of worship defined life. However, it also was necessary to approach independently the questions of Jesus Christ and of salvation after the christological question had narrowed down to the matter of the relationship between God and human in his person. In short, one may say: the christological question of the early church became a soteriological one during the time of Scholasticism and the Reformation. While the theology of the East was determined by the idea that the redeeming activity of God was ultimately aimed at the divinization of mankind, Western theology paid more attention to the process of reconciliation, as represented most prominently in Anselm: "With Anselm of Canterbury there begins not only a new chapter in the history of the doctrine of reconciliation, he is the very first to develop it with rigorous cohesion."[1] In simple terms, one could say that it has to do with the question of what happened between God and Jesus Christ and how this event can be understood.

The idea of reconciliation stresses that the redemption of humankind always assumes an event that occurs between God and Jesus Christ, which is then discussed under the themes of *atonement, sacrifice, and satisfaction*. One may also suggest that if the early

---

1. So says Kirn in his survey article "Versöhnung," 560.

church was occupied with the question of "Who was Christ?" it is now occupied with the question: "How does God's salvation reach us? What has God done for us? What is the presupposition for asserting that God has really reconciled the world to himself?" The answer has to do with the interpretation of Jesus as a sacrifice offered "for us". The person-Christology of the ancient church is thus broadened into a works-Christology.

Reconciliation as a "Gruesome" Drama? Anselm of Canterbury's Concept

In his work *Cur deus homo?* Anselm of Canterbury presented an original argument for understanding the work of Jesus Christ as mediator between God and humans.[2] Jesus reconciles by making satisfaction for the sins of humankind (voluntarily carrying away their guilt). His death was therefore "necessary," according to Anselm.

Let us visualize his train of thought: in the form of a dialogue,[3] Anselm seeks to give the Christian doctrine of redemption a purely rational basis (*sola ratione*).[4] What guided him was a problem of

2. In the history of the literature, Anselm is understood in the context of the medieval doctrine of penitence and is viewed, in part, as its representative. More recent Anselm research shows how the abbreviations and mistakes in *Cur deus homo* have become ingrained in the history of theology (compare Plasger, *Die Not-Wendigkeit der Gerechtigketi*, 39f. (in the following: Plasger, *Not-Wendigkeit*, as well as Gäde, *Eine andere Barmherzigkeit*, 13ff.). The new interpretation of Anselm, suggested by the research of Plasger and Gäde, contradicts the powerful historical-critical interpretations of F. C. Baur to A. Ritschl to A. von Harnack. The "Anselm Renaissance" (Gombocz) has shed new light on the disputed key concepts of "honor of God," "mercy and justice," "atonement and punishment" (cf. the systematic summary of Anselm literature in Plasger, *Not-Wendigkeit*, 39f.). The modern student of Anselm should not overlook the new research. I would recommend Plasger's research for deeper insights.

3. Cf. the dialogical character of Plasger, *Not-Wendigkeit*, 71f. According to Plasger, the dialogue belongs decisively to the program of *sola ratione*: "Only those who travel the thought process of Anselm can arrive at the same goal" (ibid., 74).

4. In Anselm, there is a difference between his methodological process (*remoto Christo*) and the actual conditions for faith. Karl Barth has indicated in his book on Anselm that the starting point for Anselm is always faith, the *fides*, not the *intellegere*. His goal is not to prove the incarnation of God, but "to recall what in *credo* is promised" (Barth, *Fides quaerens intellectum*, 40). Anselm

understanding. "The question upon which the entire work hangs," (I,1) is the possibility of being able to hold God's power, lowliness and weakness, his visible powerlessness in the person of Jesus of Nazareth together in thought. How does the majesty and dominion of God correspond with the story of suffering on the cross? What does the incarnation say about the being of God? In short: why did God become human? According to Anselm, people are destined for blessedness (*beatitudo*). To be alive means to give back to God what is owed him (i.e., to give him his "due"). "If angels and humans had given to God what they should, they would never have sinned."[5] So what do we owe God? According to Anselm, we owe it to God to acknowledge what he is, the Lord of Creation, and we are therefore to subject ourselves to his will.

Sin means for Anselm that the creature imbued with reason does not do the will of God, thus withholding from God the *honor* that is owed to him. Sin turns the person against God himself; they deny his lordship and thus break the first commandment. Through sin "all of human nature (is) corrupted [*tota humana natura corrupta*] and at the same time poisoned by sin [*fermentata*]" (I, 23). To what extent can sin affect God's honor? Anselm writes, "It is impossible for God to lose his honor."[6] In other words, with respect to *his person* God cannot be dishonored. Accordingly, sin does not insult God; it can, however, destroy the world order. God's intention for humans, which is to lead them to blessedness (*beatitudo*), has been foiled. Thus, with respect to *his works*, God is dishonored. *Nonne abstulit deo, quidquid de humana natura facere proposuerat?*[7] God and human, creator and

---

recognizes a posteriori: faith is not the goal in the answer to the question of *Cur deus homo*, but its precondition. The certainty that faith is present is now sought by understanding: *Si possum intellegere quod non dubito* (If I am able to understand what I do not doubt) (II, 18). Compare to the relationship of *fides* and *ratio* Plasger, *Not-Wendigkeit*, 57–64; Wirsching, "Gottes Heilstat und menschliche Freiheit," 75f.

5. *Si angelus et homo semper redderet deo quod debet, numquam peccaret* (I, 11).

6. *Deum impossibile est honorem suum perdere* (I, 14). On the interpretation of the "honor of God" of Baur, A. Ritschl, and von Harnack, cf. Plasger, *Not-Wendigkeit*, 88f.; Wenz, *Geschichte der Versöhnungslehre*, 1:45f.

7. I, 23: "Did he not take from God all that which God proposed to do with human nature?"

creation are thought of as existing in an indissoluble relationship[8] also thought of in legal terms as a contractual relationship that humans unilaterally break. In so doing, humans ultimately dishonor themselves as God's partners. If they do not honor God—that is, follow the first commandment—they destroy their own future in community with God.

Anselm also addresses God's possible reactions to sin. Citing the Augustinian distinction between power and justice, he rejects the notion that the just God could get rid of the devil with a simple powerful act. Furthermore, he disputes the basic assumption of the theory of redemption that the devil has some kind of right on the human being (I, 7).[9] Rather, God's justice demands a response to sin. Accordingly, disregarding or passing over sin is not an option. That kind of mercy would allow sin to remain intact as the destruction of the order and beauty of creation. Justice and injustice would then both be equally valid before God. Therefore, if God wants to make humans ready again for community, God must purify them, indeed free them from sin. Forgiveness alone cannot lead humans out of injustice into justice.[10] "I see that a different mercy [*aliam misericordiam*] must be sought" (I, 24). This connects with the historically determinative formula that has been abbreviated as *aut satisfactio aut poena* (either satisfaction or penalty) (I, 13, 15, 19). Here, penalty would mean leaving sinners to their own devices and accepting their unilateral termination of the contract, giving them up as lost and deserving of death (as a result of *sin*).[11] However, this goes against the divine plan of salvation, the aim of which is the *beatitudo* of human

---

8. The different legal versions that have been represented in the Anselm research have been treated by Wenz in *Geschichte der Versöhnungslehre*, 1:42-55, esp. 45f.

9. For Augustine, the devil is—as with Origen—a vehicle for implementing God's justice. He is given the right of punishment; in order to revoke it, God allows the innocent man Jesus to be delivered over to him. In that the devil exercises his conferred justice over Jesus, he puts himself in an unjust position and thus forfeits his right.

10. "Cheap grace," in addition, contradicts the being of God, since every characteristic of God must, according to Anselm, be identical with God's self (See *Monol.* XVII; *Prosl.* XII).

11. "The punishment," in the interpretation of Gunther Gäde, "consists in the loss of eternal blessedness" (*Eine andere Barmherzigkeit*, 94).

beings. God holds fast to his covenant. Community with God can thus not be reestablished "without satisfaction, that is, without freely willed removal of guilt."[12]

How can a human being imprisoned in sin get rid of guilt by her own free will *secundum mensuram peccati* (according to the measure of sin) (I, 20)? Everything that he achieves is something that he already owes to God. Thus, a being that is higher than the human being must deliver satisfaction. Hence: on the one hand, the human being *must* remove the guilt, one the other, God alone *can* accomplish satisfaction. It follows that the subject of the work of reconciliation must necessarily be the divine-human Jesus Christ (II, 6 and 7). That is why God became human. God became human, but without sin. He could go into death *of his free will*—since he was without sin (see above, the Chalcedonian decision). The sinless one does not die; he cannot die. Since Jesus, the sinless one, does not deserve death but goes into it of his own free will, we behold in him the required superior achievement that achieves *satifactio*. The death of Jesus was "necessary" for the purification of mankind, because it required something that was far greater than the abundance of human guilt. Thus, the necessity (*necessitas*) is in relation to human beings. The death of Jesus is the sufficient basis for the salvation of humankind. In faith[13] humans partake of the divine-human one (*fructus et retributio suae mortis*; II, 19), in order then to follow his example of complete righteousness (*imitatores*; II, 19). In such following, humans acquire the eternal blessedness predetermined for them. They may—indeed, they must—let themselves be represented by Christ. Why did God become human? Because only thus can reconciliation be accomplished. And God desired this reconciliation because he wanted to keep his covenant with human beings.

Anselm conceives of the divine-human relationship as a quality of relation. Reconciliation is about a juridically ordered relation that humans unilaterally disregard. This break is not ignored; Christ reestablishes the lawful order. "Here God's mercy is clearly not perceived

---

12. *Tene igitur certissime quia sine satisfactione, id est sine debiti solutione spontanea* (I, 19). "Therefore hold [to it] all the more surely, because without satisfaction, that is, without payment of debt on one's own." Latin translations by Roy A. Harrisville Sr. here and in following.

13. *Credere*: I, 20, 25; *fiducia*: II, 19.

of as disrupting the justice juridically understood, but that it carries it out to the letter."[14] A "cheap grace" is ruled out: a simple "forgive and forget" cannot reestablish the relation with God. *Humanity has not only sinned, but is imprisoned in sin.* Consequently, this requires the vicarious representation of Christ. "And only now can we discern what it has cost God for humans to be reconciled."[15]

Aut poena aut satisfactio is not an alternative in the sense of a legal course of action. God does not weigh the balance and emerge as the punitive judge. For the alternative "death or blessedness"[16] in relation to the fate of humanity has already been decided always in favor of *beatitudo*.[17] The issue, instead, is to demonstrate the appropriateness of the atonement that makes possible a new beginning with human beings and reestablishes the community of God. It is *therein* that God proves his righteousness. "Accordingly, the idea of God's reconciliation with himself is correspondingly affiliated with the idea of God's reconciliation with the world."[18]

The Humanist Contradiction—
Reconciliation as a Generous Act of Forgiveness!

Already one generation after Anselm of Canterbury an entirely different concept was moved to the center as a model for developing a concept of reconciliation: instead of satisfaction there is love.[19]

---

14. Ott, "Anselms Versöhnungslehre," 190. (The citation also points out that from a Protestant perspective, the concept of justice must not necessarily evoke the chain of associations of "Catholic doctrine of penitence," "synergism," etc.).

15. Plasger, *Not-Wendigkeit*, 171 (with explicit reference to Bonhoeffer's "Nachfolge"; cf. Bonhoeffer, *Discipleship*, 43–56.)

16. Thus does Plasger translate Anselm's phrase *aut satisfactio aut poena* (ibid., 122).

17. Even where hypothetical punishment is taken into consideration, it does not describe an action of God (in the sense of legal options for action), but rather an "absence of action."

18. Wenz, *Geschichte der Versöhnungslehre*, 1:49.

19. To what degree Abelard's concept of love includes an assessment of Augustine is ambiguous in the literature. F. H. Kettler proceeds from a "shortening" of Augustine in Abelard's concept of love ("Versöhnung dogmengeschcihtlich," 6:1374.)

Whether Peter Abelard actually can be considered the personal "antipode" to Anselm is disputed in the literature.[20] But there is no disagreement that his version of reconciliation, which he essentially developed from his interpretation of the Epistle to the Romans,[21] is in essence a counter-concept to the *Cur deus homo*.[22] For Anselm the law-fulfilling action of Jesus in his "state of self-emptying" (*status exinanitionis*) results in the act of satisfaction on the cross (and thereby acquired its actually meaning). For Abelard, on the other hand, it is Jesus' humane behavior during the time of his earthly existence that manifests God's love, which, in return, arouses love in human beings and separates them from sin. Reconciliation is therefore the effect of the over-flowing love of God in the person of Jesus Christ. In short, one could say: Anselm's work-Christology is replaced in Abelard by a person-Christology.

"How horrible and unjust it is," says Abelard with reference to Romans 3:24, "that someone's innocent blood should have been exacted as a kind of ransom or that it should have pleased someone one way or another that an innocent person should have been killed, much less that God should have considered the death of his Son so agreeable that through it he became reconciled with the entire world!" In Abelard's view, there was not the slightest necessity for God to save humanity through the incarnation and the death on the cross of Christ.[23] Instead, he says, "After the forgiveness of sins, on account of which they were punished, there is no reason why they should be punished any further on account of them." After all, Christ already forgave sins prior to his death. The cross thus means: God has "bound us even more closely to himself through love." "Our redemp-

---

20. Cf. Plasger, *Not-Wendigkeit*, 68, on this discussion.

21. Especially impressive are his comments on Rom 3:22ff., in *Petri Abaelardi opera*, 204ff. I cite in the following from the German translation of G. Sauter, *"Versöhnung" als Thema der Theologie*, 62–69. On the theological-historical categorization of the commentary on Romans, cf. A. Ritschl, *Die christliche Lehre von der Rechtfertigung und Versöhnung*, 1:48–52.

22. The only agreement between Anselm and Abelard may be seen in their unconditional denial of any claim the devil has over people.

23. In the interpretation of Rom 3:25, Abelard asks rhetorically, "Why, I ask, was it necessary that for our redemption God's Son, after he took on flesh, had to suffer so much fasting, abuse, flagellation, humiliation, and finally the most harsh and shameful death . . . ?"

tion is thus the highest form of love given to us through the Passion, which not only frees us from the servitude of sin, but gains for us the true freedom of the children of God..." Faith therefore has an ethical quality for Abelard, because this "love has been spread out in us." He argues that because "God in Christ has united himself with our nature and through his suffering has proven his highest love for us ... we are, on account of Christ, equally linked with God as with our neighbor in an indissoluble bond of love." Love for God opens up for believers—and only for them—interpersonal forgiveness.[24]

The humanistic concept of reconciliation with its mutually interconnected main aspects—the humanistic image of God and the moral image of the human being—has experienced a renaissance, stimulated, among others, by presuppositions in the intellectual history of the Enlightenment and later of liberal theology that were favorable to this humanistic concept.

The further development of Abelard's idea of reconciliation in the Enlightenment was in accord with its basic corresponding anthropological concepts. Reconciliation is a "subjective" event: it comes to fruition *in the human being*. Anselm's doctrine of reconciliation lacks "attentiveness to human autonomous activity."[25] An "objective" understanding of reconciliation as an event *external to the human being* was no longer comprehensible under the changing conditions of intellectual history. The "talk of a wrath of God assuaged through the blood and the sacrifice of Christ" was seen as "an accommodation to the 'fanciful notions' of Jewish sacrificial theology and practice."[26] "Moreover, the argument was advanced that the individual cannot in principle be represented by another against the allegedly biblical teaching of the *satisfactio vicarii*."[27] Gunther Wenz argues, "For modern theology, the doctrine of the appropriation of salvation became one the most important levers with which to pry

---

24. "... for this reconciliation concerns only those who believe in and expect it." Abelard does not recognize a "general reconciliation." Reconciliation is an exclusive thing that is limited to the faithful.

25. Wenz, *Geschichte der Versöhnungslehre*, 1:54.

26. Ibid.

27. Ibid.

the entire pre-modern doctrine of reconciliation from its moorings and to subject it to a basic re-organization."[28]

Thus, for example, the Socinians, a movement in the second half of the sixteenth century influenced by Fausto Sozzini, negate the triune nature of God: "Fulfilling the law is something everyone has to accomplish on his or her own, as her or his very own obligation and deed."[29] Guilt or merit cannot be transferred; forgiveness and satisfaction are mutually exclusive. The fact that sin is always already forgiven, needing neither atonement nor allowance of atoning acts on the part of humans, has theological consequences. Karl Heim characterizes this in his phrase "the God of the Enlightenment takes guilt lightly."[30] In the theology of Rationalism, Christ is primarily "truly human" and accordingly the divinity of Jesus is contested. "In Socinianism, salvation is ultimately a matter of good will; people essentially have to achieve their salvation themselves. Christ only serves as a good role model for them."[31] The change in contrast to Abelard is clearly evident in this Christology. For the Socinians, Christ is not actually the revealer of the love of God, but a "form of manifestation of divine teaching,"[32] to which one should now connect.[33]

In addition to Scandinavian theologian Gustaf Aulén,[34] it was the Berlin Luther scholar Karl Heim who traced the further development of this view into the nineteenth century, emphasizing again its contrast to Anselm. "For the humanizing, ethicizing doctrine of reconciliation, which came into being with the Enlightenment and was extended and significantly changed by Ritschl, reconciliation is

---

28. Ibid.

29. Ibid., 125.

30. Heim, "Die Haupttypen der Versöhnungslehre," 311.

31. Wenz, *Geschichte der Versöhnungslehre*, 1:127.

32. Ibid., 114.

33. A renewed shift of emphasis in the subjective type takes place (as the result of the rediscovery and new interpretation of Anselm by Hugo Grotius) in pietism and neology. Cf. the informative section in Wenz, *Geschichte der Versöhnungslehre*, 1:149ff. Steiger ("Aufklärungskritische Versöhnungslehre," 129) draws a direct line from the Enlightenment neology (A. H. Niemeyer), with its juridical-ethical appeal "to apply oneself to one's job and duties as Jesus did as martyr," to the vocational ethics of Albrecht Ritschl.

34. Cf. Aulén, "Die drei Haupttypen des christlichen Versöhnungsgedankens."

not a juridical act, but a moral process within human beings through which the tarnished relationship of man to God is reestablished."[35]

The concepts "justification" and "reconciliation" in the title of Albrecht Ritschl's book *The Christian Doctrine of Justification and Reconciliation* are intended, as Ritschl states in the foreword, "to eliminate the assumption of a change in God through Christ, from wrath to grace."[36] The material criterion that marks Ritschl's value-judgment of the course of history is "the distinction between an ethical and a juridical concept of reconciliation."[37] In comparing Anselm and Abelard, Ritschl rejects juridical categories of presenting reconciliation found in the church's doctrine and sides with Abelard.[38] The ethical structuring of the idea of reconciliation is bound up with the basic theme of his investigation, which is the superiority of the

---

35. Heim, "Haupttypen der Versöhnungslehre," 305. In contrast to Heim, Gustaf Aulén (*Haupttypen des Versöhnungsgedankens*, 529) sees F. Schleiermacher also along the lines of subjective types of reconciliation. The fact that Schleiermacher is seen as the "renewer of the Abelard type of teaching in the modern history of Christian teaching on reconciliation," says Gunther Wenz, is "in so far correct as Schleiermacher shares with Abelard the basic aversion to Anselm in particular and to the juridical version of the doctrine of reconciliation in general" (*Geschichte der Versöhnungslehre*, 1:372). Reconciliation, according to Schleiermacher, operates so that believers no longer see the evil in their lives as punishment for sin; the experience of divine grace leads to the overcoming of the consciousness of sin; cf. Schleiermacher, *Glaubenslehre* (1830), §100f., esp. §104. On Schleiermacher's concept of reconciliation in the framework of history the Christian doctrine of reconciliation, cf. the comprehensive treatment in §11 of Wenz, *Geschichte der Versöhnungslehre*, 1:366ff. O. Kirn ("Versöhnung," 569) offers a differentiated assessment of Schleiermacher's version of reconciliation, in which he, on the one hand, finds fault, "that it relegates reconciliation behind redemption, relates it to the evils of the world thereby mistaking the decisive weight of the forgiveness of sins." On the other hand, he cites as "worthy" the "strong unity" "with which Christ's person and work are linked. In so doing, Schleiermacher has overcome the isolating treatment of the individual sides of the work of salvation . . . and given the impetus for basing the doctrine of reconciliation on inner experience and historical perception."

36. A. Ritschl, *Rechtfertigung und Versöhnung*, 1:2.

37. Wenz, *Geschichte der Versöhnungslehre*, 1:23. On A. Ritschl's concept of reconciliation in the history of the Christian doctrine of reconciliation, comprehensively §14 in Wenz, *Geschichte der Versöhnungslehre*, 2:63ff.

38. Cf. A. Ritschl, *Rechtfertigung und Versöhnung*, 1:31f.

moral spirit over the natural world.[39] The reality that dawned with the Gospel asserts "that as a spiritual entity the human being has a higher value in God's eyes than does the whole world of nature."[40] According to A. Ritschl, reconciliation can never be grasped in terms of juridical categories. God just cannot be conceived of in objective categories. Rather, reconciliation refers to the priority of divine love over against any impulse of wrath. In the preaching of Jesus, God reveals himself as loving unconditionally and as being ready to forgive; attributes that were sealed through Jesus' death. Human beings are reconciled with God when they become conscious of the justification already accomplished.

The humanistic idea of reconciliation used against Anselm's position is advocated with modifications in the twentieth century.[41] In contrast to nineteenth-century presentations, reconciliation is no longer "only about an inner disposition of humans," but finds its significance "above all in its social-political dimension."[42] Altogether, the observed switch from the motif of the individual's change of consciousness to the program of social-political reconciliation encompasses the span in which the criticism of Anselm's work-Christology encounters us.

In the end, these attempted solutions are not convincing. The basic humanistic model of Christology presented in disparate formulations does indeed address how reconciliation comes about among us, on earth. And so, Abelard's "very big question" loses none of its significance: "*what* actually *is* our *salvation* through the death of Christ?"[43] How is the "advent" of reconciliation in us conceivable? What does it mean for human beings and *their* forgiveness? How does it relate to the interdependence between the love of God and the love of the neighbor? The core problem, however, lies in the basic christological decisions that precede the concept of reconciliation and the anthropological consequences that follow from it. One

---

39. See Günther, *Die Entwicklung der Lehre von der Person Christi im XIX. Jahrhundert*, 312.

40. A. Ritschl, *Rechtfertigung und Versöhnung*, 3:577.

41. See Seiger, *Versöhnung, Gabe und Aufgabe*.

42. Ibid., 162.

43. Interpretation of Rom 3:25. Cited in Sauter, *"Versöhnung" als Thema der Theologie*, 64. Emphasis added.

could argue that reconciliation calls to discipleship. Vicarious representation does not lead to moral laxity. But at the same time, the assumption that in principle human beings cannot be represented vicariously before God, as the Enlightenment (especially Kant) vigorously asserted, can be maintained only with a relativized concept of sin. "Thus, the problem of reconciliation has lost its sharpness and deepest seriousness," as Gustaf Aulén noted insightfully.[44] The theologian Bernd Seiger[45] aptly summarizes this ambivalence: "the main characteristic" is "the relatedness of the idea of reconciliation to the world and the hope for progress in ethical behavior," on the one hand; while on the other hand, "the understanding of reconciliation as the establishment of community with God through Christ's atoning suffering" has receded.

A Possible Solution: Accept Reconciliation as a Precious Gift! The Doctrine of the Threefold Office within the Horizon of Reconciliation

The question of "why the Father sent Christ and what he has brought us" (Inst. II, 15) was answered by the Genevan reformer Calvin in terms of the threefold office of Christ:

- the prophetic office of the earthly Jesus as proclaimer of the kingdom of God;
- the royal office as the spiritual reign of peace of the exalted one;
- the priestly office in the power of which—according to Anselm—Christ in his death offers the sacrifice for the reconciliation of the world.

Calvin's concern was to describe the true basis of salvation in discussion with the Roman Catholic Church.[46] With that his description shows from the outset that the work of Christ encompasses *more*

44. Aulén, "Die Drei Haupttypen des Versöhnungsgedankens," 529.
45. Seiger, *Versöhnung, Gabe und Aufgabe*, 162.
46. Karl Barth has incorporated this teaching impressively and given new emphasis to some aspects, especially with respect to the prophetic and kingly office. Cf. Kühn, *Christologie*, 319f.

than *death and sacrifice*. It has to do with his preaching during his earthly ministry, the interpretation of his suffering and death, and with the proclamation of his resurrection and ascension. Taking up the New Testament testimony, Calvin tried to develop the activity of Jesus under these three aspects and not to confine it to atonement. It is interesting that each of these three aspects—Jesus as revealer, redeemer, and lord—was upheld from early Christology onwards albeit with different emphasis. Every aspect relates itself, each in its own way, to the other two. While in the Old Testament kings, priests, and prophets were anointed, Jesus Christ, as the anointed one, unites all three offices in himself: that of prophet, priest, and king.

Calvin gives the attempt to depict the saving activity of Christ in terms of the theory of the three offices determining significance. That theory had already been outlined in the fourth century by Eusebius of Caesarea and was formulated by Anselm in the eleventh century in his version of the "priestly office." For the central question of how the "advent" of God's reconciliation with us, humans beings, can be thematized is answered: the salvation wrought by Jesus Christ is the breakthrough *into life*. Here, life, in its most complete sense, means that alienation from oneself, from God, and from fellow human beings has come to an end and that this life, constantly falling back into a state of alienation, is continually given life anew as a gift. This life is visible in the activity, suffering, and life of Jesus Christ and is perceived in the manner of each of the three offices. Here, human beings find their "center"—in Jesus Christ.

There is much to be said in favor of interpreting the three aspects with Calvin on the basis of what the Reformation called the "office of mediator" (*opus mediatoris*).[47] This office consists in Jesus Christ reestablishing the community between God and humans that sin disturbs, indeed, destroys. This involves that

1. in Christ God manifests himself to humans as one in community with them (the concept of revelation—prophetic office);

2. in Christ God reestablishes community with the lost human beings (the concept of reconciliation—priestly office);

3. in Christ humans are freed to live life in community with God (the concept of redemption—kingly office).

47. Compare the following to Härle, *Dogmatik*, 316 f.

CHRISTOLOGY IN A WORLD OF HUMANISM

It is not by chance that the concept of reconciliation is also central to what has come about for the good of the world and for humanity on account of Christ. If we put reconciliation at the center, then questions emerge: how can reconciliation be discussed without narrowing it to the aspect of "satisfaction"? How is it conceivable that in Jesus Christ the divine and the human come together *for our salvation*? How does what was said about the *person* of Christ in the fourth and fifth centuries fit in with what was said concerning his *work*? And finally, how can we talk responsibly today about the reconciling activity of God in Christ?

In light of the crisis of how to understand salvation in the late Middle Ages, Martin Luther, in his theology of the Reformation, was the first to succeed in radically emphasizing the saving nearness of God in Jesus Christ as the core idea of reconciliation. The decisions of Nicea and Chalcedon and their development by John of Damascus and the subsistence Christology of the Middle Ages were, in his opinion, valid assumptions, but have been strained to the limits of the possible.[48]

A theme of Luther's theology is saving nearness to God in Jesus Christ; he makes the humanity of Jesus Christ his starting point: in a world of anxiety and sin, God himself is near in the activity and the suffering of Jesus Christ in his humanity, near *for our salvation*. Here God lets himself be grasped and achieves certitude. In order to articulate this nearness, Luther risks correcting the established theory of the hypostatic union: if God is close to us in the humanity of Jesus Christ for our salvation, then he is also near to us here and now for our salvation. But then the humanity of Jesus Christ after the ascension can be locked away in a heavenly room as scarcely as the divinity

---

48. Thus, regarding justification, Luther can say, in opposition to Latomus in 1521 (WA 8, [36]43-128): "He who wishes to discuss sin and grace, law and gospel, Christ and man, in a Christian way, necessarily discourses for the most part on nothing else than God and man in Christ; and in doing this one must pay the most careful attention to predicating both natures, with all their properties, of the whole Person, and yet take heed not to attribute to this what belongs exclusively to God or exclusively to man. For it is one thing to speak of the incarnate God, or of man raised up to God, and another to talk simply of God or of man. So also sin apart from grace is different from sin in grace, so you can picture grace and the gift of God as having become sin in the one case, and sin as having become grace in the other as long as we are in this world, so that because of grace and the gift, sin is no longer sin." Luther, *Against Latomus*, 257.

of Jesus Christ can be closed off from suffering. Rather, it is near to us today as humanity in union with the *logos*: in the word of promise and in the Lord's Supper as the meal of the promise. The nearness of Jesus Christ is the nearness of the *logos* as it is that of the human being Jesus in the one person of Jesus Christ. Where Jesus Christ is, there he is also according to his humanity. Thus, within the framework of the theory of the hypostatic union, the humanity of Jesus Christ himself is connected, as genuine humanity, directly and not merely indirectly via the person to the Godhead. The understanding of heaven and of Jesus Christ seated at the right hand of God is, therefore, freed from all spatial conceptuality: heaven is not a defined place, but the realm of God's salvation. The place at God's right hand is not a place in heaven, but the perception and recognition of ruling authority through Jesus Christ in the wholeness of Son of God and Son of Man. The human nearness of God in Jesus Christ is a saving nearness effective for everyone personally.

The interpretation of Luther presented here presupposes that what we say about the person of Christ needs to be interlocked with what we say about his work—a quite decisive presupposition! Johann Anslem Steiger elaborated this inner connection in Luther and got to the point of it when he sought to show that Luther's doctrine of the "communication of proper qualities" (*communicatio idiomatum*) between the divine and human nature exists in an internal relationship with his doctrine of the "happy exchange."[49] The latter says: Christ takes on our sins through his death and in exchange gives us his righteousness. "God's reconciling act binds Jesus Christ with our lot. What was *meant for us* is laid *upon him*—sin—so that *in him* we become what we can never procure on our own: God's righteousness."[50] The doctrine of the *communicatio idiomatum* says that there is an exchange of qualities between the divine and the human nature. Hence, with respect to Christ, it can also be said that the human being Jesus has created the world. Or: God was born and lay in the manger, and even: God suffered and God died. Luther placed

---

49. On Luther's linguistic-theological insight into the meaning of metaphorical speech for life in the happy exchange and in the struggles of Christ, see especially "On the Freedom of the Christian" (12th section), WA 7:20–38, esp. 25f.

50. Sauter, "*Versöhnung" als Thema der Theologie*, 26.

"the offensive and scandalous (1 Cor 1:23; Gal 5:11) dimension of the incarnation of God and of his humiliation to the point of death on the cross."[51] For Steiger the doctrine of the *communicatio idiomatium* is for the doctrine of the person of Christ what the "happy exchange" is for the doctrine of the work of Christ. Thus, the "happy exchange" is to a certain extent the continuation of the *communicatio idomatum* in the area of soteriology. "In that God became a human being, God not only takes on a human nature, but the entire *humanitas* and appropriates everything that comprises humanity: mortality, indigence, sin and depravity, even the full range of God's judgment of wrath on humankind. In the opposite way, however, humankind receives all that actually is apportioned to God alone: righteousness, eternal life, and glory."[52] In summary, Luther has "utilized [Christology] in the service of soteriology, in that he read both doctrines synoptically."[53]

Even though we are still in the midst of the theology of the Reformation, we are in effect already at the key question, namely, how can we today speak responsibly of the reconciling activity of God in Christ? That this is the case is closely tied to the line of thought that can be drawn from Luther to Dietrich Bonhoeffer.[54] This line extends from affirming the christological dogma (while simultaneously maintaining an existential point of departure), and the tight connectedness of the person and work of Christ, to the insistence on the incarnation and corporeality of the community of humanity with God and, finally, to the centrality of Christ for how humans relate to the world and for all of Christian ethics. In his interpretation of Luther, Bonhoeffer is concerned with more than a causal connection between Christology and the doctrine of reconciliation. "It rather has to do much more with the convergence of the doctrines of the person and of the work of Christ, because they are defined through *one single* and central essential hallmark. With Luther this is called '*communicatio idiomatum*' and the 'happy exchange,' whereas in Bonhoeffer it is called the 'pro-me-structure.'"[55]

51. Steiger, "Die communicatio idiomatum als Achse und Motor," 4f.

52. Ibid., 5f.

53. Ibid.

54. In relation to what follows from her, see also the inspired contribution of Lehmkühler, "Christologie."

55. Ibid., 59.

In accordance with Luther, Bonhoeffer, in his lectures on Christology, defines the *person* of Christ in terms of the "pro me." Soteriology and the doctrine of the person are closely interwoven when Bonhoeffer asks, "By virtue of what personal ontological structure is Christ present to the church? If one answers, by virtue of his God-humanity, that is correct but still needs explication. It is the '*pro-me*' structure. The being of Christ's person is essentially relatedness to me. His being-Christ is his being-for-me. This *pro-me* is not to be understood as an effect that issues from Christ or as a form that he assumes incidentally, but is to be understood as the being of his very person. The very core of his person is '*pro-me*.'"[56] Is it possible in this interpretation by Bonhoeffer to distinguish correctly between the person and the work of Jesus? Apparently not, since the person of the Son is defined as being by nature there for the human being. "One could also say that the 'happy exchange' is the essence of Jesus Christ. The Son of God is defined as 'pro-me'; he takes my place. Vicarious representation and God-humanity condition each other."[57] A further parallel to Luther is evidenced where the pro-me structure extends itself into the life of the congregation and into the life of Christians in that they are "a Christ" to their neighbors. Ethics emerges from Christology. "Christ's vicarious representation also leads to the vicarious-representative action of Christians—an idea that in Bonhoeffer's reflections on the 'responsible life'[58] plays a fundamental role. Here one can draw lines up to the well-known formula of the church for others."[59]

The close interweaving of the doctrines of Christ and reconciliation in Luther and Bonhoeffer makes it possible to relate God's reconciliation and the world's real irreconcilability one to the other. Bonhoeffer's (and Luther's) idea of the Christian, who becomes "a Christ" to their neighbor,[60] implies that one can exchange places with those who bear suffering and are beset with sore temptation. Bonhoeffer reflects on this thought in the Tegel letters when he exhorts

56. Bonhoeffer, *Berlin, 1932–1933*, 314.
57. Lehmkühler, "Christologie," 63.
58. Bonhoeffer, *Ethics*, 257–61.
59. Lehmkühler, "Christologie," 66.
60. The theological problem of this formula consists in the preservation of the difference between Christ and us in relation to his reconciling activity.

us "to share in God's sufferings at the hands of a godless world."[61] However, this also means that those reconciled in Christ—whether at the time of Luther or of Bonhoeffer—will not have the "burdens" they bear in their historical situation taken from them. They are not spared suffering as they accept their responsibility. History itself doesn't provide ways to "hammer" historical events "back into shape." In this interpretative context, Christology links God's suffering and the experience of alienation from God on the part of those who "sym-pathize," who "suffer with" the suffering.

In light of this, reconciliation is more than and something different from a corrective of the consciousness (as is the case with Albrecht Ritschl, Friedrich Schleiermacher,[62] and in general in the humanistic sense of reconciliation). It is more and something different, because the solution to the conflict between God's justice and his love of creation and of humankind does not occur in the believing subject, but *in God himself* (as Anselm of Canterbury correctly underscores). It is also yet again more and something different in Anselm, because reconciliation does not somehow remain closed "in itself," leaving the reconciled "untouched," but draws them in and, (as Bonhoeffer points out in reference to reflections of Luther's) actually lets them "participate" in it.

The dispute about the "juridical " or "humanistic" understanding of reconciliation is not only about whether the biblical accounts are sufficiently addressed. Rather, the dispute, both historically and currently, was and is much more about the unvarnished perception of the rift, the deep disorder that burdens the world. "*Nondum considerasti, quanti ponderis sit peccatum*" is how Anselm put it to his interlocutors. The history of the freedom of humankind has evolved into a history of guilt, which has a very real, daily discernible, and even "objectively" destructive meaning for both people and the world, with individual, political, and cosmic dimensions. The Apostle Paul rightly addresses God's ongoing judgment in which God has "given humans over" to the designs of their hearts (Rom 1:24). In the context of the significance of Jesus' death, we had already referred to God's judging activity to which Jesus submitted himself

---

61. Bonhoeffer, *Letters and Papers from Prison*, 480.

62. Cf. Schleiermacher, *Christian Faith*, vol. 2 (1830), §100, Heading, §101, Heading and Section 2.

in his suffering and death. It was a situation of heightened rebellion against the one who had come in the name of God to forgive sins and to preach reconciliation. Speaking of "reconciliation" is to say that through Jesus' fate, the judgment of God was broken through and guilt was taken away. "Father forgive them, for they know not what they do" (Luke 23:34)—forgive them, for they are the tools of the judgment that hangs over the world. The aim of the work of reconciliation through Jesus Christ is to insert, with the removal of guilt, an opposing force into this "metaphysical" conflict between the will of the Creator and the creation that has been distorted through guilt. It is the force that makes forgiveness possible even where it fundamentally exceeds human measurement, creating an inner connection between the reconciliation already accomplished (breaking through and lifting the nexus of guilt) and the signs (or symbolic adoptions)[63] of this reconciliation to be seen and to be advanced in the midst of political and cosmic reality.

Accepting the Challenge of "Humanism": The Doctrine of the Reconciliation of Jesus Christ as the End of all Gruesome Sacrifices

There is an obvious similarity the theme of "reconciliation" shares with other christological themes: when looked at from Scripture, one encounters it always in numerous images and concepts—such as sin-offering, vicarious representation, redemption—all of which attempt to describe the meaning of the saving activity of Jesus Christ "for us." But can one argue, as does the *humanistic-enlightened argument*, that we should do without certain "gory" ideas of Christ such as sin-offering and the like? Do ideas like these even bring Christology as a whole into disrepute? Is it possible to believe that a loving God would cast his Son as a player in such a gruesome drama?

---

63. In my study *The Political Dimension of Reconciliation*, I have—in response to the political upheaval in South Africa and Germany—searched for what Peter L. Berger calls "signs of transcendence."

A Note of Encouragement

- The Christian idea of sin-offering is significant in that it puts a stop to every form of sacrificial cult. For the idea of sacrifice, which is criticized in the *humanistic-enlightened argument*, presupposes that in order to reestablish the relationship, the death of the guilty party or of another life in its place is demanded. The idea that sacrifice is necessary, prevalent in many religions (and in their secular political offshoots!), is radically overcome in the Christian faith in the notion that in Jesus' death on the cross God sacrificed himself for the sake of lost humanity.

- In view of this paradoxical exchange of roles, through which God himself is the sacrificial victim and in which the idea of sacrifice is fulfilled in an utterly matchless way, one can assert that Christian soteriology is not regressive, but emphatically futuristic: in the death of Jesus Christ any institution of the cult of sacrifice, be it religious or political, is brought to an end and in a certain regard is itself "sacrificed."

- This line of thought makes plain that God does not let an innocent person simply suffer and thus prove himself to be cruel, inhumane, and unacceptable for humanistic-enlighenment thinking. *God does not let Jesus suffer, but God himself suffers* in that he has bound himself to human nature in order, in Jesus Christ, to reconcile the world to himself (something that Bonhoeffer, drawing on Luther's Christology, speaks of as "the suffering of God in the world").[64]

- Sin-offering cannot be replaced by a mighty act of forgiveness or a generous act of God's love, which, at first glance, may seem to

64. Daub, *Die Stellvertretung Jesu Christi*, 516, refers correctly to something unclear in Bonhoeffer with respect to the relationship of the suffering of God and of Christ. The fact that God suffers in the death of his Son can mean two things: "the Father suffers alongside the sufferings of Christ." It could also mean: "Jesus, the Son of God become man, suffers; namely, God suffers—as the second person of the Trinity, in that God suffers as the Son of God become human." According to Daub, it must remain open which nuance comes closer to Bonhoeffer. In my view, the first option is quite unlikely, because Bonhoeffer in his lectures on Christology rejects the modalistic idea of *patripassianism*. To the extent that Bonhoeffer follows Luther's teaching on the *communicatio idiomatum*, all the other versions are possible.

be "more humane." For *one* question still remains: what happens with transgressions that love covers over or deems unimportant? In the act of forgiveness, they would merely be "covered over," but not eliminated. They would still shine through—something that is not, in my opinion, a very "humane" idea. The final overcoming of sin—not just a provisional "putting aside"—occurs in the suffering and death of Jesus Christ. From now on, sin can no longer separate humans from God. Even more: the pain of slander and betrayal is neither ignored (as in the motto "forgive and forget") nor put back through an act of retaliation on the sinner. Rather, in Jesus Christ, God "works out" and suffers this pain *in himself.* He (Jesus) is "made to sin for our sake" (2 Cor 5:21).

- "Cheap grace" is ruled out; a simple "forgive and forget" cannot re-establish the relationship to God. *Humans have not only sinned, but are caught in sin.* Consequently, they need the vicarious representation of Christ. And, according to Bonhoeffer, the one represented in this vicarious representation is humankind as such.[65] And again it is humankind to whom Christ's vicarious representation is addressed, to be accepted, and to be lived by. This must be clarified in view of the *humanistic, enlightment objection*: the representation spoken of here is in reference to the relationship between God and humans disrupted through sin. Representation in the relationship between one human being and another, disrupted (through ethical guilt), does not appear at all in Anselm. There is no such thing in a court of law as a christologically-grounded vicarious representation. There, people must *de jure* answer for their deeds. The theological doctrine of reconciliation is suited neither to an ethical lack of responsibility nor to immaturity (in things *coram mundo*).

- In expanding upon this idea, vicarious representation (*coram mundo*) does not mean that, in reference to the historical situation, Jesus Christ suffered (for us) what we (due to his representation) would not have to suffer. Not only does the indisputable experiences of many Christian people go against this idea: even

---

65. It was above all Bonhoeffer's experience in the opposition against Hitler that allowed him to believe in a vicarious representation even beyond its acceptance in faith. See Daub, *Die Stellvertretung Jesu Christi*, 512f.

after Christ, Christian people are not spared suffering, illness, or death. According to Luther and Bonhoeffer, and against the background of the doctrinal idea of the unity of the person and work of Jesus Christ—or also of Christology and the doctrine of reconciliation—this is what is meant by conformity to Christ: "Christians stand by God in God's own pain."[66] Those people who do not evade this are called Christians. The taking on of responsibility is "participation in the sufferings of God in the world."[67]

---

66. Bonhoeffer, *Letters and Papers from Prison*, 461.
67. Ibid., 480.

6

Christology in a World of Gender Equality

How Can the Man Jesus Save?

From a feminist perspective, traditional Christology is of no use to liberation theology—for society globally and for women in particular. Yes, the Bible does show Jesus standing on the side of the suffering and disenfranchised, and also on the side of women. In addition, feminist (re)reading of Scripture paints a different portrait of Jesus. At the very least, any talk of God as Father and of Jesus Christ as Son reflects patriarchal social relationships. That is true also for the further development of the ancient church's Christology. A male savior is out of the question for women, since liberation cannot be expected from a man (Daly). For that reason it is necessary to develop a person-Christology without gender difference whatsoever (Schüssler Fiorenza).

Basic Outlines of Feminist Theology and Ethics

The feminist argument that Christology serves no liberation-theological purpose presumes a particular idea of the *liberation* of human beings, specifically of women, through the encounter with the gospel of Jesus Christ as the saving love of God. Here, liberation is understood as a very "real," intra-historical process, measured by the standards of the world, a liberation from oppressive, patriarchal structures. It is not contested *that* there is liberation through Jesus Christ; rather, the *how, what,* and *when* of this liberation is contested. The gospel, the good news of God's redeeming love, which in Jesus Christ makes human beings into something that they cannot make of themselves—namely, a human being loved by God—seeks, without any doubt, to liberate. None less than Luther addressed this liberation of the human being before God impressively in his "manifesto on freedom."[1]

Feminist liberation-theological re-readings challenge the dimension of liberation. To what does liberation and refer and not refer? What does it include and not include? Which relationships does it have in mind? My relationship to God? Or that to the church as the community of saints? Is it the social and political conditions in which we live? Or the cosmos beyond individual or existential categories? What is included in the liberation to which the good news of Jesus as the Christ testifies? When can we expect this liberation? In the here and now, or will there be redemption only at the end of time?

In christologies of social liberation, and especially feminist theology, counterquestions are raised about "classical" issues, such as the question about the unity of the divine and the human in the *man* Jesus Christ (person Christology), or about the allegedly *wrathful Father-God* (work Christology), who can be reconciled only by the sacrifice of his son. In addition, it is obscure in terms of *liberation* theology how the arrival of the reconciliation of God and humans accomplished in that manner can be considered as liberating from oppressive political and social reality.

With the *feminist objection* we enter in some manner into the third large area of the topics that every Christology has to deal with. There are the interpretations of the divine origin of Jesus, *God's incarnation* and the mystery of his person related with it (the "who question"), and there are those of the *suffering and death* of Jesus of Nazareth and the work associated with that (reconciliation). In the topic of "liberation" the light shines on Easter, the *interpretation of the resurrection* as victory over the death and all that brings

---

1. See Luther's "Von der Freiheit eines Christenmenschen," WA 7, (39), 41–73, StA I, 260–309 (English: Luther, *The Freedom of a Christian*). On the meaning of the Lutheran difference, see Härle, "Gott fürchten und lieben. Martin Luther und die Kunst lebenswichtiger Unterscheidungen."

suffering in this world (redemption). How is Jesus' proclamation of the coming reign of God related to the early Christian proclamation of Jesus as the Christ? An intellectual link to what the pre-Easter Jesus has proclaimed is forged. If the talk of liberation is connected more closely with the term "redemption" (than with reconciliation), then it becomes clear already terminologically that "liberation" (like "redemption") has eschatological meaning. The reference is to an event which here and now is knowable only in fragments and whose completion is still pending.

The specifically feminist approach to liberation is structurally connected in the christological argumentation to approaches of political liberation theologies.[2] The starting point for feminist liberation theology is the attempt to gain in light of Jesus of Nazareth viewpoints for a new understanding of the holistic character of being human and the aesthetic that goes with it, as well as for a non-repressive form of religion and, foremost, for an ethic that is no longer defined by male ideas of power. Although one can no longer speak in the singular *of the* feminist theology,[3] there are common ideas that may be regarded as a unitary front against the Christology of the ancient-church Christology that nearly all representatives of the feminist approach find unusable for liberation theology. Naomi Goldenberg[4] speaks of religiosity as an intra-psychic process for discovering the goddess as a psychic image that allows women to be self-affirming. Christa Mulack[5] sees the female as a superior principle, the male as needing redemption and, against this background, Mary as a demonstration of female power and the untouched integrity of human

---

2. Here we mention the central political-theological position of a "theology of hope" (Moltmann), Latin American liberation theology (Leonardo Boff), and so-called black theology (James Cone); cf. the brief overview by Kühn, *Christologie*, 71, 77.

3. Here cf., among others, Hopkins, *Feminist Christology*; Scherzberg, *Sünde und Gnade in der feministischen Theologie*; Strahm and Strobel, *Vom Verlangen nach Heilwerden*; Strobel, "Feministisch-theologische Kritik an Kreuzestheologien."

4. Goldenberg, *Changing of the Gods: Feminism and the End of Traditional Religions.*

5. Mulack, *Die Weiblichkeit Gottes. Matriarchale Voraussetzungen des Gottesbildes.*

nature. Heide Göttner-Abendroth[6] assumes the historicity of a matriarchal epoch when peace with utopian qualities prevailed, thereby advancing female power as a symbol of the divine as well as a model for human action. Elga Sorge[7] stresses that the Christian message of redemption should not be distorted by a dispiriting doctrine of sin and a male-sadistic symbolism but should lead to self-love and self-acceptance through a life-loving female spirituality. Starhawk (a.k.a. Miriam Simos)[8] sees in the goddess the symbol of the cosmos, of the equilibrium of nature and of social relationships. Finally, Mary Daly[9] understands sin as the alienation of women from their essential being and thus from participation in the divine, so that the "self-becoming" of women is the path to God and redemption. All of the above authors of this aesthetic-mystical direction of feminist theology share the idea of an absolute immanence of the divine and unity of the divine and the human.[10]

- There is in a real sense no separation from the divine (and thus no sin for the sake of which God would have had to become human/male to reconcile humankind), because the goddess represents the cosmos and the self. This unity is sought through mystical or ritualistic means. In short: knowledge of self is knowledge of God and as such the highest spiritual task.

- Redemption is understood as the process of becoming whole. Wholeness is holiness and a hallmark of the divine, to participate in which is our task. In this wholeness, all polarities, including good and evil, are united. Reconciliation is thus participation in this wholeness.

- In the positions outlined above, the liberation-theological dimension consists in the joining of the symbol of the goddess to the fate of women because it furthers female self-affirmation and the peaceful, social, and ecologically harmonious organization of society.

6. Göttner-Abendroth, *Die transzendente Göttin. Prinzipien einer matriarchalen Asthetik*.
7. Sorge, *Religion und Frau. Weibliche Spiritualität im Christentum*.
8. Simos, *Die Kraft der großen Göttin*.
9. Daly, *Beyond God the Father: Toward a Philosophy of Women's Liberation*.
10. Cf. here the comprehensive analysis of Scherzberg, *Sünde und Gnade*.

If one looks at these interpretations against the background of the classical christological ideas of the person and work of Jesus Christ, one will notice how completely separated they are! The unity of God and the human that, according to the aesthetic of feminist theology, is based in absolute divine immanence, leads to the dissolution of the reality of sin and grace, and thus to the loss of the *eschatological hope* for a *new* world, whose newness is qualified precisely in that it has yet to come. Lucia Scherzberg puts it in a nutshell when she queries "whether" such feminist theology "in fact serves human and, in particular, female liberation."[11]

Another basic line in feminist theology can be understood more readily within the framework of Christian dogmatic substance: the basic ethical orientation. We can place here those reflections of woman-theologians that address the role of humans in redemption, the relation between justification and sanctification as well as more specifically christological questions. Judith Plaskow[12] underscores from her gender-specific perspective that the doctrine of justification reflects men's experience in depicting sin essentially as pride. It is time, she writes, that a doctrine of sin be developed that includes women's experience as being inferior and self-deprecating. Similarly, a doctrine of grace is needed that thematizes the unfolding of the self as "participation" in God's creative dealing with human beings. Carter Heyward[13] understands sin as the absence of relationships, as the refusal to accept the communion with God as female co-creators; she therefore enjoins all to live mutual relationships with one another and with God. Rosemary Radford Ruether[14] understands sin essentially as the dualistic separation of things that should belong together, as well as the manifestation of unjust, sexist structures, and views redemption as the elimination of all differences and the transformation of sexist structures. Elisabeth Schüssler Fiorenza[15]

---

11. Ibid., 186.

12. Plaskow, *Sex, Sin, and Grace: Women's Experience and the Theologies of Reinhold Niebuhr and Paul Tillich*.

13. Heyward, *Und sie rührte sein Kleid an. Eine feministische Theologie der Beziehung*.

14. Ruether, *Sexism and God-Talk: Toward a Feminist Theology*.

15. Schüssler Fiorenza, *In Memory of Her: A Feminist Reconstruction of Christian Origins*.

regards sin as the prevention of the experience of God's presence, and presents grace, goodness, and reconciliation (incarnated in Jesus-Sophia) as the basis for the possibility of the egalitarian ethos of the Jesus movement of the early days of Christianity; she concludes accordingly that the church makes itself culpable of the sin of sexism wherever it denies this egalitarian ethos and with it God's grace and goodness. Dorothee Sölle[16] seeks to bring the political dimension of sin into focus and thereby shift the accent from Christology to the theology of creation. Finally, Catharina Halkes,[17] (similar to creation theology) places God's acts of blessing at the core of her understanding of reconciliation and, in so doing, assumes a continuity of grace which regards the aspect of holiness rather than justification as central for women: essentially, sin is the repudiation of one's destination for (continuing) co-creation. All these authors share the view that Christology—as far as it is taught and developed at all—must be entirely in the service of fundamental statements about the co-working of humans in redemption, the primacy of holiness (before justification), and the acceptance of the immanence of God. Clearly, what is regulative is the idea that Jesus Christ is the paradigmatic human being and thus the symbolic representation of grace and redemption: he is the immanence of God.

If one views these ideas against the background of classical Christology and the doctrine of God, at least two questions emerge:[18]

- What kind of anthropology is behind these arguments? All authors stress, despite their affiliation with disparate churches and denominations (!), human responsibility as co-creators and cooperators with God; the moral ability to make decisions and the actions of humans are assessed very optimistically. Indeed, while most of the arguments indicate that God's mercy precedes moral action, the danger of moralizing sin and redemption cannot be entirely ruled out. If one considers the Lutheran idea of justification of the sinner through the accounting of *the alien righteousness* of Jesus Christ, then it becomes apparent that most of the proposals fall short of the explosive controversial

16. Sölle, *To Work and to Love: A Theology of Creation*.
17. Halkes, *Suchen, was verloren ging. Beiträge zur feministischen Theologie*.
18. Cf. Scherzberg, *Sünde und Gnade*, 118.

theological power of the idea of the *cooperatio* as well as its attending theological problem of the intertwining of soteriological and ethical paradigms.

- What pneumatology directs feminist liberation theology? If the theme at the forefront of Christology is the immanence of God and the "arrival" of reconciliation under the aspect of sanctification—then should the reflection of the Holy Spirit not move to the theological center of this "arrival" of reconciliation (as it is indeed characteristic in the political liberation theology of Jürgen Moltmann)? Unfortunately, with some exceptions,[19] a pneumatological reflection is lacking that could appropriately locate the immanence of God theologically and illuminate the feminist theological horizon.

Liberation Theology as a Challenge to Christology: Between Legitimate Concerns and Ethical Misinterpretations

It is a basic concern of liberation theology to avoid speaking of God's reconciliation "docetically" that is, in disregard of the concrete, actuality of the world that is often characterized by oppression, exploitation, and hatred of women. This concern is not only justified, but, in view of the challenges of theology today and the church in a globalized world, also necessary. Feminist theology—like liberation theology in general—addresses the central question of every political ethics: How can Jesus Christ be conceptualized, taught, and spoken of today so that his freeing message "catches on" in political and social reality?

The didactic legacy of Christology provides very little insight into this question. The basic problem that the arguments of feminist theology we have discussed illustrates is, first of all, that neither in the traditional position of person Christology (in the creed of Chalcedon) nor in works Christology (e.g., Anselm) are liberation theological questions dealt with at all (and thus no direction is given by which to find answers). In fact, the social dimension of reconciliation

---

19. Primarily Scherzberg, ibid., 241–46.

with its "liberating" arrival in political reality was, in the strictest sense, not a theme in the larger debates of the ancient church or in the church of the Middle Ages. In this regard, critique of the efforts of feminist liberation theology is also always a critique or at least a questioning of the theological project itself.

The leading question remains and challenges Christology: How can the liberating activity of God in the world be talked about without either relativizing it (reconciliation as limited to the space and time of the NT), or individualizing it (reconciliation as a mere contract between God and humans) or moralizing it (Jesus as the model to follow)?

But the legitimate concern to thematize the arrival of reconciliation also in the female experience of the world is burdened with a considerable theological mortgage in its programmatic implementation. The basic outlines of feminist theology sketched above are deficient in a number of aspects and problems are compounded rather than offering workable solutions.

- The *image of God* presented in the aesthetic form of feminist theology, in its mystical-apersonal conceptions, is barely or not at all compatible with the biblical image in Jewish-Christian tradition.

- The *epistemological path* of feminist theology is not always clear. Does it proceed (inductively) from the experience of women to the image of God or (deductively) from the revelation of God in Jesus Christ to the human being? One could ask somewhat pointedly whether the image of God—at least in the aesthetic-mystical direction—is not, in the sense of an *analogia entis*, "constructed" from a current image of women such as that based in the myth of holism. (This is reminiscent in some ways of the epistemological path of the "liberal life-of-Jesus research," which ended, as is known, in the reconstruction of autobiographical "images of Jesus.")

- The *eschatological* tension in which liberation expresses itself between reconciliation and redemption, between the *already now* in faith and the *not yet* in looking forward to the new world, is eliminated in favor of an immanently conceived Christ (male) or Christa (female). The unity of the divine and the human, which according to the feminist theological aesthetic is grounded entirely in the absolute divine immanence, leads to the complete disintegration of the actuality of sin and grace, as well as the loss of eschatological hope for a truly new world.

A New Solution from Political Ethics: Liberation Theological Impulses from Dietrich Bonhoeffer Ethics

How can one, in line with the decisions of the Chalcedonian Creed, speak appropriately of God's condescension, even his "suffering," his nearness, without sliding into heterodoxical conjectures or ethical circumlocutions? If one places feminist theology in the framework of the previously discussed christological questions, then one can discern at least four conceivable ways to understand feminist liberation theology. One can view it as a counter project to the "individualizing" and "patriarchal" work-Christology of Anselm (→ section *a*); one can view it in line with the idea of ethical reconciliation (→ *b*); one can categorize it as a Sophia-project outside the Jewish-Christian idea of God (→ *c*); or one can make the attempt to analyze the legitimate concern of liberation theology in view of Bonhoeffer's political ethics and relate it back to the church's Christology (→ *d*).

a) Liberation Theology as a Counterproject to Anselm of Canterbury, or, the Juridical Model Is No Solution

If one disregards the historical chronology of its development, one may view Anselm's work-christological project in terms of its subject well as a critical-conservative counter concept to all of liberation theology. As stated earlier, reconciliation for Anselm of Canterbury is essentially a process between God and humans. The question as to what possible social, political, and feminist liberation theological implications can result from this reconciliation in Christ lies outside this horizon of inquiry. For Anselm, reconciliation as a process between God and humans has no social implications. It is clear that this important soteriological concept comes up short with respect to feminist-theological questions about the "arrival" of this reconciliation for liberation in the here and now.

The basis for this can be found in the following: on the one hand, the focus of feminist liberation theology lies in the pre-Easter personage of Jesus of Nazareth—his liberating message and his loving activity—and not in the work of Jesus Christ fulfilled through obedience. In general, post-Easter Christology and with it the doctrine of the two natures are suspect of patriarchal dominance: here Christ is nothing short of a patriarchal symbol (R. Ruether).[20] Likewise, the traditional theology of the cross is judged critically, according to which Jesus had to die a bloody sacrificial death in order to placate the wrath of the Father. The death of Jesus is rather a consequence of his life and activity on earth which Jesus himself did not intend, but must be seen as a "tragedy and a prophetic unveiling of the nihilistic disposition of those who deify power."[21] However, at the same time, his death is an expression of the suffering of God, who participated in the humiliation of Jesus.[22] The resurrection is an event in the memory of the disciples that makes clear to them that Jesus' ministry has not perished. "In the experience of a group of mourning disciples something happened that opened up a liberating new revelation of life" and symbolized the "dynamic efficacy of God."[23] A unity of the divine and the human in Jesus is rejected, at least in the sense of a manifest duality of above and below; rather, God is to be found implicitly in the ministry of Jesus.

b) Liberation Theology in Line with the Humanist Model of Reconciliation, or, a Radical Solution through the Moralization of Christology

Liberation-theological approaches of ethical-feminist reflection are reminiscent of the "humanistic model of reconciliation" both in its portrayal of Jesus and its basic anthropology. It has been stated several times that the pre-Easter Jesus, his message and activity is at the center of feminist theology, especially in its ethical tendency. The

20. Ruether, *Sexism and God-Talk* (German edition, *Sexismus und die Rede von Gott*, 145 ff.).
21. Hopkins, *Feministische Christologie*, 72.
22. Ibid., 75.
23. Ibid., 88, 91.

hermeneutical approach of this "Christology from below" sets out from the experience of women today; the image of Jesus is defined and "conceived anew"[24] from here. The preferred reference text is the Gospel of Mark.[25] "Not the person, but what Jesus was about"[26] is at the center, that "universal happening of power and love," which was initiated by the message and activity of Jesus of Nazareth and in which we are now to join. Away with every patriarchal person—or work—Christology and back to Jesus! That is how one could sum up this position pointedly.

The "Christology of below" has a corresponding optimistic image of human beings quite commensurate with the "humanistic model of reconciliation." Lucia Scherzberg summarizes it thus: "The woman-theologians of the ethical orientation place human freedom at the center, which they understand as self-determination, the ability to relate to others, independence and dependency.... That is why the affinity between the ethical feminist theology and a doctrine of grace that stresses human freedom and cooperation is not a product of chance, but almost unavoidable. For a pessimistic view of the human ability to desire and to do the good, or the emphasis on the inability of human beings to contribute something to their salvation and the corollary that striving to do so is sinful, can do little that is beneficial for ethical consciousness and ethical praxis."[27]

According to feminist theologian Carter Heyward, this ethical praxis of humans, has to be oriented by the "liberating praxis of Jesus."[28] Jesus appears here as a person in whom the power of justice is visible; namely, a justice that is expressed as responsible love in the sense of just relations, in which "freedom and the striving for happiness not only for us, but for all"[29] becomes real. Christology is to be centered on "the ability for relationships and community as the wholeness-creating, healing core of Christianity," which could also

---

24. Heyward, *Und sie rührte sein Kleid an*, 75.

25. See Hopkins, *Feministische Christologie*, 137 ff.; Heyward, *Und sie rührte sein Kleid an*, 83ff.

26. Citations from Klinger, *Christologie im Feminismus*, 167.

27. Scherzberg, *Sünde und Gnade*, 238.

28. Heyward, *Und sie rührte sein Kleid an*, 41.

29. Ibid.

be described as a "Christa/Community."[30] Jesus can and will awaken in us this kind of power of justice—namely, in the sense of being able to realize just relationships of love. Feminist theology in the ethical orientation must be seen and judged in the context of a correlation between divine and human love. However, the danger of an emphasis on ethical activity is the "moralizing of religion." Again, Lucia Herzberg: "Feminist theology must be on guard here not to find itself having landed in the camp of civil religion in the worst sense. On this question the Lutheran tradition of justification as an accounting of the alien (i.e., not our!) righteousness of Jesus can serve as a steady corrective of feminist theology."[31] Wherever this occurs, genuine feminist theological approaches become available.[32]

This "alien" righteousness corresponds to the view of the ancient church that Jesus of Nazareth can never be comprehended by human perception, be it that of a man or a woman—he remains basically "alien" to us. Jesus, although a human being like us, remains always wholly other. The discussion of the historical Jesus showed precisely that we do not know this Jesus at all—accordingly, every son-father, mother-daughter analogy falls short. Jesus, the human being, who can truly love, is different—different than we are; he transcends any image that we make of him, whether patriarchal or feminist.

In summary, it is possible at this point to say two things: if Anselm's model falls short in the area of social ethics, then the humanist model falls short in the area of soteriology. If, in the "juridical model," the "arrival" of the reconciliation brought about by Christ is not addressed at all, then it is not clear in the feminist version of the humanistic idea of reconciliation whether and to what extent God reconciled the world with himself in Jesus Christ at all and, in so doing, brought salvation to human beings. If, with Anselm, reconciliation is reduced through individualizing to a relationship between God and humans, in feminist Christology redemption is conceived

---

30. A term used by Nakashima Brock, cited by Klinger, *Christologie im Feminismus*, 165.

31. Scherzberg, *Sünde und Gnade*, 238.

32. See Moltmann-Wendel, "Gibt es eine feministische Rechfertigungslehre?", who sees the message of justification as a special message for women, in that women can accept themselves as a good creation—as good, whole, and beautiful.

of as a social-ethical and not a soteriological process and is correspondingly relocated to this world.

c) Liberation Theology without Connection to the Christian-Jewish Tradition, or: Solution through a New Image of God[33]

Woman-theologians of the aesthetic orientation place the immediacy and power of religious experience at the center. The result of this is, as with Gnosticism and mysticism, an emphasis on the unity of God and humans, and a high estimation of symbolic and mythical forms of expression and a strong tendency to eliminate the difference between humans and God. Concentration on experience and its symbolization means that religion is radically subjectivized. The spiritual longing that is depicted in these feminist ideas is not necessarily Christian, but points to a deficiency of meaning in the modern world as much as it points to a deficit of experience of Christian theology and practice. The anxiety that exists in the conditions of modern life is countered with the help of myth. Dealing with myth is an aesthetic process, that is to say, it is a faith without faith, a relation to reality but not as reality but as possibility.

In the mythical model, too, hope is ultimately relocated to this world—in Bonhoeffer's words, in the "penultimate things." A prospect for actual liberation from historical suffering cannot be found here. This view of God lacks eschatology as well as ethics. But does this not put into question the uniqueness of Christ, as intended in the testimony of the New Testament and in the Christian confessions? But the image of God, eschatology, and ethics form a unity in classical Christology. Accordingly, these three dimensions are the "crunch points" of feminist liberation theology. All criticism notwithstanding, the struggle for an appropriate understanding of liberation that is a continuos thread through the conceptions of feminist theology remains an important question. "Classical" Christology is reminded that there is a social and the political dimension to the healing being and action of Christ, which has been more of a marginal issue for the church's person- and work-Christology.

---

33. Cf. for the following Scherzberg, *Sünde und Gnade*, 239.

d) Liberation Theology on the Foundations of Church Christology? Some Solutions in connection with Bonhoeffer

If one wants to address the concern of liberation theology, and of feminist theology in particular, namely, the "entry" of divine reconciliation into the midst of the political and social reality of the non-reconciled, of oppression—especially of women—of enmity, torture, and human rights violations, and to do so meaningfully, one needs to heed the following. The Christian religion must not be moralized (by fading out soteriology), the Christian doctrine of God should not be abandoned as such (by an embrace of mythical-gnostic trends), nor must one be "fixated" on a soteriological doctrine of reconciliation (by fading out the social-ethical dimension of the Christian idea of reconciliation).

I think that traditional person- and work-Christology gives a sufficient number of perspectives to thematize the liberating activity of God in Jesus Christ and to work toward a liberation theology on an "orthodox foundation." I see potential connecting links for this above all in the line from Martin Luther to Dietrich Bonhoeffer drawn in the previous chapter. In both interpretations of the Chalcedonian Creed, the interdependence of the doctrines of the person and work of Christ was discernible and were treated thematically under the terms "happy exchange," *communicatio idiomatum*, and the "pro-me structure."[34] Now the path is to lead further into ethics, which, for Luther as well as Bonhoeffer, grows from Christology. "Ethics from faith" one could say with loose allusion to the pluralism debate. Furthermore, Christology is the model for anthropology. For Bonhoeffer (as for Luther[35]), Christ's vicarious representation continues in the

---

34. The similarly possible line from Calvin's teaching on the prophetic as well as the royal office to that of Karl Barth's teaching on the royal reign of Christ cannot be pursued further here, and is merely touched in connection with the remarks on Bonhoeffer. Cf. Klappert, *Versöhnung und Befreiung*.

35. In his writing on freedom, Luther says, "See, according to this rule the good things we have from God should flow from one to the other and be common to all, so that everyone should 'put on' his neighbor and so conduct himself toward him as if he himself were in the other's place. From Christ the good things have flowed and are flowing into us. He has so 'put on' us and acted for us as if he had been what we are. From us they flow on to those who have need of them so that I should lay before God my faith and my righteousness that they may cover and intercede for the sins of my neighbor which I take upon myself

life of the congregation and of Christians; yes, their very lives become the actions of vicarious representation. To become a "Christ" to the neighbor always means also to step in and change places with those who are suffering and sorely troubled, to participate in God's suffering in the world. However, this is only conceivable against the background of a strong idea of the incarnation. If the son has truly become flesh, is natural life not valued in an unprecedented way? "All earthly-ties, indeed, Luther's zest for life, have their origin here as do concern for one's neighbor and attention to the concrete cares of life."[36] For Bonhoeffer—and with him for political ethics—the nexus of these thoughts provide for making a connection to liberation theology's core concept of this-worldliness. I would like, therefore, to discuss Bonhoeffer's concept of the "penultimate things" in more depth.

Excursus on Bonhoeffer

Bonhoeffer's essay "Ultimate and Penultimate Things" in his *Ethics* is an attempt at a new interpretation of Lutheran political ethics, as it is primarily articulated in the "doctrine of the two kingdoms." The dynamic distinction between "ultimate" and "penultimate" things opens a perspective on liberation as a real event in space and time—and the (neo-Lutheran) fixation on "thinking in two spheres" is overcome.

For Bonhoeffer, the "penultimate" describes[37] everything in need of redemption, justification, and liberation: suffering, oppression, and being guilty. "The penultimate is not a condition in itself; it is a judgment by the ultimate on what has gone before." In terms of categories of time, it means that the penultimate is "never something present, but always something already past." It *has become* the penultimate. As a result, says Bonhoeffer, a dynamic emerges that overcomes thinking of liberation, justification, and reconciliation as static categories. In place of the (neo-Lutheran) "order," there emerg-

---

and so labor and serve in them as if they were my very own. That is what Christ did for us" (WA 7, 37, 32–38, 2) ("Freedom of a Christian," in Lull, *Martin Luther's Basic Theological Writings*, 623)

36. Lehmkühler, "Christologie," 67. On "Erdverbundenheit Luthers" cf. Elert, *Morphologie des Luthertums*, 1:393–406.

37. Following citations from Bonhoeffer, *Ethics*, 159f., 150f.

es the idea of a (dynamic) "process." For Bonhoeffer this means first that the penultimate must be "preserved" for the sake of the ultimate, for the justifying Word reaches us only in the penultimate. *Becoming guilty just as becoming free is something one can only become in time.*

The "ultimate things" are also "the *temporally* ultimate word." Something penultimate always precedes it: "some action, suffering . . . hoping—in short, quite literally a span of time at whose end it stands." The word as temporally "ultimate" means a "complete break" with the penultimate. "There is a time of God's permission, waiting, and preparation; and there is an ultimate time." In terms of liberation theology: there is a time of injustice, of powerlessness, of forbearance, and of waiting for redemption. Where the ultimate "judges and completely breaks" the penultimate, there is the "time of grace."

In terms of our discussion of the problem, this means that we cannot count qualitatively on a *more* in addition to the last word, which is Jesus Christ (as in the mystical-aesthetical expansion of a patriarchal image of God), nor on a temporal *more* in addition to the ultimate word, which is Jesus Christ (as in looking for a future time of mercy that a moralizing religion could bring forth). An idea of God determined feministically is excluded just as is any kind of undetermined futuristic optimism in progress. Both reckon with a qualitative and temporal "more." Where the liberating, justifying, and reconciling word reaches the penultimate, it engages it and changes it entirely and completely.

Bonhoeffer says "no" to the question of "whether one can live by the ultimate alone, whether faith, so to speak, can be extended through time."[38] Rather, it seems to him that faith is "the last moment of a time span or of many time spans." Faith is not "realized daily and hourly." Rather, it must "walk the long way through the penultimate for the sake of the ultimate."[39] But this also means that in the "real"

---

38. Ibid., 151f. Following citations, ibid.

39. Bonhoeffer asks, for example, why it is that "when facing someone grieving deeply over a death" he often decides on a penultimate action, namely, "human solidarity" instead of "biblical comfort." It is a possible indication, as he reflects on the situation, that there is no "controlling the situation spiritually" for every occasion and that indications of the ultimate can also be found in conciouslyly remaining in the penultimate (ibid., 152f.).

world, salvation can "become only *partially* real" and at the same time threatened "by its opposite."[40]

But the decisive message of a political ethics influenced by Bonhoeffer is this: something of the luster of *the ultimate* can indeed be seen *in* the penultimate *in* moments of its *complete break*. I have already mentioned the *signs of transcendence* in connection with Peter L. Berger, which prompt *this* recognition.[41] It becomes suddenly clear that this is how we must see the situation from God's perspective. This is the "moment of the Holy Spirit" (P. Lehmann). The recognition-releasing "occasion" can be a sign, a "moment of revelation,"[42] like a handshake between two feuding people, or a gesture symbolizing the end of oppression of women. For those who have experienced them, such "interruptions" are a ground of hope; they become immanent and are remembered, so to speak, "on the tracks of time."

To cite a biblical example: that God is a true God who keeps his covenant is an experience formed by the recollection of the (historical) liberation from Egypt. The command "remember!" is highlighted in bold relief throughout Deuteronomy. The subject of the remembrance is the slavery in Egypt and subsequent liberation by God. This unitary theme that connects the differentiated legislation of Deuteronomy, shows a "tendency leading away from all casuistry to the spiritual meaning lying behind the individual laws," and urges that we make it "subjectively present" to us and "inwardly appropriate" it.[43]

What can be said about the interruption of the penultimate by the ultimate and about moments of liberation in the midst of the unreconciled world? How can one conceive of the *coming* of the reign of God? From these questions arise impulses that take us beyond Bonhoeffer inasmuch as an overarching connection between the ideas of "interruption" of the penultimate and the activity of the Holy Spirit can be established.

---

40. Härle, *Dogmatik*, 602. Following citations ibid.

41. See Wüstenberg, *Political Dimension of Reconciliation*, 80–101 (in connection to the question of correspondence), esp. 86f.

42. Citation from D. Ritschl, "Gotteserkenntnis durch Wiedererkennen," 149.

43. von Rad, *Theologie des Alten Testaments*, 1:225 n. 79.

We can find no basic pneumatological connection not only in feminist theology; Bonhoeffer, too, did not anchor his ideas in Trinitarian theology. But it does not take much imagination to close this gap. What if Bonhoeffer had taught something other about the reign of God than that it is "imminent,"[44] that the "new creative event" "under the conditions of this world is notoriously unfinished, . . . challenged, called into question, under suspicion, contested, embattled, ridiculed"? It is helpful in this regard to see the Holy Spirit "as the universal power of the presence of God," whereby creatures act "in the field of his eminence" although "not at all always in conformity with its intent."[45] This important distinction pneumatologically anchors the difference between teleology and eschatology: it is those few luminous moments in which the purposes of the creatures are in conformity with the purposes of the Creator. Openness according to Bonhoeffer's meaning of the term is to allow oneself to be "interrupted" by this "emanating power"; to be "open" to it and to "believe." God reveals himself in that he breaks the penultimate (for example, the nexus of "what happens to you is the result of what you do" that is so calamitous for political liberation) and creates hope, which can include new ways of acting. Whether God's spirit was "at work," or whether we are dealing with an activity in conformity with the orientation and domain of his power, we come to *re*-cognize in an "occasion." We need to find out whether such "occasions" (e.g., "free self-restraint"[46]) can be found in the reality of politics. The example that comes to mind is how Nelson Mandela dealt with his erstwhile political enemies after his release from prison. Are those moments of forgiveness and testimony to the aforesaid "self-restraint" insofar as they are a voluntary refusal to retaliate in kind"?[47]

For Bonhoeffer, the ultimate and penultimate things do not separate out into two static areas; thus any "thinking in two spheres" is excluded. He rather conceives of an internal "relationship" between the ultimate and the penultimate. The freeing, redeeming,

44. This and following citations: Welker, "Die evangelische Freiheit," 68-73.
45. Bernhardt and Link-Wieczorek, *Metapher und Wirklichkeit*, 446.
46. Welker, "Das Reich Gottes," 508.
47. Donald Shriver, in Huber, ed., *Schuld und Versöhnung in politischer Perspektive*, 27, is among "the proponents of forgiveness," who, among other things, "reject retaliation in kind." See also Shriver, *Ethic for Enemies*.

and justifying word and the fallen world remain in mutual relation. Bonhoeffer picks up an idea present in the Lutheran doctrine of the two kingdoms but obscure in its reception history. He uses this idea to access pivotal aspects of the Reformed "doctrine of the royal reign of Christ." In Bonhoeffer's reflections on the term "relationship" are points of contact with the Reformed tradition, especially Calvin. One the one hand, in his ethics Bonhoeffer wants to ward off certain neo-Lutheran tendencies, such as the demand to strengthen the differentiations that the doctrine of the two kingdoms makes to separate and isolate what belongs together, the result of which is "that the Gospel differentiated from the law does not become efficacious for the formation of social and political life."[48] But on the other hand, Bonhoeffer sides with those who make allowance for the world's (relative) autonomy: the domain of secular government is viewed as "the field of cooperation between Christians and non-Christians on the basis of reason."[49] Bonhoeffer is not to be counted among the interpreters of the doctrine of the royal reign of Christ who view the state directly as an "exponent" of the reign of Christ, "as a simile and analogy of, and a correspondence to the reign of God proclaimed by and believed in the church."[50]

We follow now Bonhoeffer's line of reasoning in the context of the formation of political theory of these two doctrines: that of the "two kingdoms" and that of the "royal reign of Christ." For one, I reckon with an openness in the reasoning of political ethics according to which processes in the political reality cannot be linked so unambiguously with a Christian interpretation that the inner connection between the interpretation and the process to be interpreted would be coherent for all. For another, one should look within procedures guided by the above-mentioned openness for that recognition of Christian signs of transcendence signaling the "new world" within the political reality conditioned by a (relative) autonomy. The search for signs of transcendence—for signs of the new, liberated, reconciled, and justified world, is embedded in the eschatological tension

---

48. Rogge and Zeddies, *Kirchengemeinschaft und politische Ethik*, 33.

49. Huber, *Kirche und Öffentlichkeit*, 452.

50. Ibid. But Karl Barth also addresses the dimension of reason in the implementation of a state's ethic, whereby the state should take action and make decisions on the basis of reason.

that is appropriate to the saving activity of the triune God in the created and fallen world: God has reconciled the world to himself in Christ (2 Cor 5:19) and has snatched victory from hell (1 Cor 15:55). However, at the same time Christendom still has to wait for the new heaven and the new earth (2 Pet 3:13). One has to make allowance here that the world is not in complete correspondence with Christ's benefits; it even contradicts it often, but one must still look for signs of correspondence.

There are elements in the Reformed tradition[51] that are constructive for our exploration of the problem, such as the interpretation of the concept of the reign of God. John de Gruchy writes, in the context of the political transformation of South Africa, "The vision of democratic transformation resembles in many ways the eschatological vision of the coming reign or kingdom of God.... We know that the reign of God is not something which we can bring into being through social action, and we also know that the reign of God is always something ultimate, something beyond our achievement. At the same time, the reign of God can be anticipated in concrete ways here and now."[52] Michael Welker problematizes this "at the same time": "The coming reign of God has in common with the activity of the Spirit and the activity of the Word that it does not arrive like a train or a bus so that we could say 'now it's here,' or 'it is not here yet.' Rather, the reign of God is active already among us *and at the same* time is still outstanding. It is an entity from beyond, an entity that comes toward us from the future, and is *at the same time* in our midst, a living present. It is visible outwardly . . . in that justice and mercy bear fruit. And *at the same time* it remains hidden in the heart, in memory, in expectation. The reign of God is therefore no illusion,

---

51. On the newer discussion, cf. the volume edited by Willis and Welker, *Toward the Future of Reformed Theology*.

52. De Gruchy, "Christian Witness in a Secular State," 91. The task of the church in the new South Africa, says de Gruchy, is to warn against attempts at absolutizing the political: "Critical theological reflection on the state and the challenge of democratic transformation must . . . continually return to the prophetic source of Christian faith and its witness to the reign of God. Indeed, this provides the basis upon which Christianity must reject all absolutist political claims as idolatrous, and therefore keep the political process open-ended" (ibid., 93).

but is the form in which God, using the service of human beings, exercises his reign in this reality."[53]

Next to the differences already outlined, a constructive connection between the doctrines of the two kingdoms and the royal reign of Christ needs to be noted. In a certain respect, Bonhoeffer has anticipated the later state of the discussion in that he was open to fresh interpretations of those two models of thought. Neither does the differentiation between the ultimate and penultimate indicate that the Christian existence is split up into two areas that lack an externally perceivable unity, nor does it show tendencies of denying the worldliness of the world (such as the autonomy of domains of political life).

Bonhoeffer succumbs neither to the danger of the "neo-Lutheran" disconnecting law from morality in order to create a legal space for autonomy with its readiness to accept fluid transitions from a relative to an absolute autonomy of the law all the way to supposition of divine orders of creation,[54] nor does he give in to the other danger of conflating law and morality into one, as is the case wherever theological distinctions remain abandoned and developments in the intellectual history of the Western legal tradition that led to the consequential secularization of its religious roots remain ignored.

From Bonhoeffer's critical vantage point, two things become clear for our discussion: in the face of the danger of separating theology and law, the existence of immutable core values—such as the dignity of the human being—must be stressed; they are to be respected unconditionally, even if they cannot ultimately be defined. They mark the limit of all state power; when they are transgressed, then, from a theological perspective, the autonomy of law is at its limit. In the face of the danger of mixing theology and law, it must be stressed that the actualization of human rights is not identical with the actualization of the justice of God that is received in faith. "That is how

---

53. Welker, "Elend und Auftrag der nach Gottes Wort," 36. The connection to the above analyzed concept of process consists in emphasizing that "at the same time" does not mean "simultaneous."

54. Troeltsch, *The Social Teaching of the Christian Churches* (German edition, 500ff.) has interpreted the doctrine of the two kingdoms in the sense of such autonomy and addressed the "double morality" of Lutheranism.

the proclamation of the Gospel liberates the law to its temporality and worldliness."[55]

What Solutions Are Offered in a Bonhoefferian Perspective?

From Bonhoeffer, there are available coordinates, as it were, for a framework or conditions with which to begin formulating a "new" political ethic, which has yet to be written. The "new" consists, for one, in that the "arrival" of reconciliation is treated thematically in the indicative (not the imperative). Christ is already present in the world (long before reconciliation was made into a political demand or described as a mode of freedom); indeed, Christ has long "laid claim on the world." The issue now is the "re-cognition" of *his* way. The imperative to re-cognize Christ's way is addressed principally to believers who are to trust that Christ's reconciliation is in fact already breaking through even, and particularly, when and where the church is not at all visible. This is where the constructive potential of the so-called doctrine of the two kingdoms lies. For another, the new consists in the fact that the ethics "flows" from the Christology: where the incarnation is taken seriously, Christ is not only present "next to" the Christian, but "lays claim on" the "whole" Christian in the midst of his/her life. The Christian woman or man becomes "a Christ" to the neighbor and enters with the suffering one into a "happy exchange." Liberation Christology following Bonhoeffer (and Luther) is always both exclusive and conclusive: exclusive, insofar as the Son of God suffers (and is raised), and conclusive, insofar as Christ takes the Christian into the suffering (as well as into the horizon of the resurrection and liberation).

For the purpose of our discussion, Bonhoeffer's outline yields criteria for a liberation-theological approach that may also be of interest to the feminist-theological discussion:

- Bonhoeffer's liberation-theological statements should be understood as a further development of Luther's theology of the cross against a *theologia gloriae*. Liberation in the here and now

55. Huber, *Kirche und Öffentlichkeit*, 450f. (in connection to Luther's interpretation of the Magnificat).

is basically a spiritual category. The incarnation, God's entering into the world in space and time, always means a "hiddenness" of God, which does not suit the liberation-theological concept. For God's appearance in the world in the suffering and crucified Christ is contested in the world, remaining inscrutable to non-believers. But for believers, God's suffering in the world is disclosed, indeed, gives rise to a christologically qualified consolation in knowing that God participates in the suffering of the yet un-reconciled world. This participation is not a revolutionary one, but a quiet, healing one. It lets Christ's suffering enter life and gives those who suffer a horizon of meaning. But that horizon is not to be confused with a direct determination of meaning, because there is no Christian meaning for the fact that human beings are made into victims. Rather, it is the very meaning*lessness* of every sacrifice after that of Jesus Christ that raises the question *why*?

- Liberation must not be interpreted christologically to mean that suffering will hastily come to an end. Rather, Christians are called to suffer with Christ's suffering in the world. Redemption presents a span of time, and also one of suffering. Liberation has to be waited for. It is a contingent event from God. Here there is no *co-operatio*. Liberation is an interruption from God, itself a circumstance of eschatological hope; any attempt to force redemption is christologically untenable and doomed to failure—the teaching of many secular-utopian offshoots to the contrary.

- Where liberation is thought of as coming from God, it cannot be about the construction of a new, reconciled reality, but about the re-cognition of signs of this new world liberated by Christ, the great counter-design in the midst of the old, un-reconciled world. Feminist theologian Lucia Scherzberg writes, in the context of the liberation-theological horizon of "re-cognition," "If talk of the activity of the Holy Spirit in history is taken seriously and if the Spirit is not indifferent to oppression and injustice, then it should be asked whether the churches could not recognize the work of the Holy Spirit in the liberation of women."[56]

---

56. Scherzberg, *Sünde und Gnade*, 245.

CHRISTOLOGY IN A WORLD OF GENDER EQUALITY

- The political reality of the suffering of humans, of men as well as women, such as is the case in totalitarian systems, and the theological perspective on the sufferings of Christ, are thus not ontologically communicated through the use of the same word "suffering." The positive connection—or the "permeability" of political into theological ideas of suffering and vice versa—itself produces a christological perspective: namely, where the reconciling account of Jesus liberates people to attend to the sufferings and hopes of the past. From this perspective, synthetic connections are possible in the process of remembering the *memoria passionis, mortis et resurrectionis Christi*. The story of Jesus Christ's sacrifice then breaks indirectly into the history of sacrifice. Remembering does not receive its actual theological climax in memorializing what is morally horrible. The stories evoke something different than nightmarish oppression in view of the morally incomprehensible. They harbor hope. It is the hope that God has not abandoned the world, but leads it to what it is determined to be through the hope of change that he brings about and that radiates into the here and now today.

- A positive example of liberation theology: the forums of the Truth and Reconciliation Commission (TRC) in South Africa and other so-called truth commissions offer victims of totalitarian arbitrariness the invitation for renewal, acceptance, and relief. Where this relief succeeds, no new human sacrifices are produced and the *circulus vitiosus* of violence is broken. The end of the "sacrificial cult" is truly reached. In individual cases, the following happens during a hearing: the victims of egregious human rights violations let go of their burden, that is, their powerlessness and their pain, and they gain a voice: telling the story *un*burdens. The suffering was not in vain; it is heard. The past can thus become a "saved" past. In terms of content, stories are about the abuse of human dignity. What is told is the story of degradation.

Here we can observe an interesting symbolic interaction. In the process of the hearings, a fate is acknowledged. Who does the acknowledging? Who contributes to the re-establishment of dignity? In the first instance it is those gathered in the hearing rooms of the Truth Commission: the victims' stories do not fade away, but are, as said above, heard. In the process of listening the stories resound; a symbolic "exchange" takes place. Suffering is relinquished and, through the participation of the listeners, taken up: a new perspective on life is won. In the perspective of reconciliation, victims can see themselves as they are seen by God, namely, as human beings with dignity. The acting subjects *now* are not the victims, but the participants in a TRC hearing. *They* represent the new society in which human dignity is respected. It is *they* who echo the stories and contribute to dignity being respected once again. *They* make things right.[57] Is not this symbolic implementation, characterized above as a hallmark of Luther's Christology, involved in the processes of political reality? The new society gives back something that the previous society had taken away. The experienced injustice of degradation is exchanged for symbolic processes of rightfulness emerging that contribute to this degradation being morally overcome and healed. We must ask whether we can recognize in this "past-political exchange" between listeners and narrators a Christian-anthropological transformation of human beings in the "happy exchange."

- It is true that political action remains distinguishable "from the expectation of salvation by faith that transcends the world, the power of freedom, that no one can appropriate."[58] And yet, the formulation of liberation-theological criteria in connection with Bonhoeffer cannot stop at a simple acknowledgment of this difference. There is a spiritual recognition of the already reconciled world in the midst of political reality. If one takes seriously Luther's concept of ubiquity, one can also say: Christ is "everywhere" at work, and precisely also in the sufferings of the

---

57. Particularly impressive are the indications of symbolic processes in this interdependence, which accompany the South African as well as the parliamentary reports of the Enquête-Commission, "Treatment of the History and Consequences of the SED Dictatorship in Germany." At the entrance of the victims, all those gathered *rise*. This gesture is a symbolic representation of the conviction that the dignity of the person is inviolable and must be respected, even though it has been trodden underfoot.

58. Rendtorff, "Die Zweireichelehre oder die Kunst des Unterscheidens," 53ff., n. 60.

world. In line with Bonhoeffer's distinction between "ultimate and penultimate things," structures have to be provided by social ethics that make possible the breaking in of the ultimate into the penultimate. The "ultimate" must be able to reach the "penultimate" in space and time. The way must be prepared. In terms of our example, a space must be created in which victims can tell their stories and people can listen to them.

Taking on the Challenges of "Feminism": Christology Is Useful for Liberation Theology!

What are we to say now? Is traditional Christology of no use to liberation theology? Does it even thematize the arrival of the reconciliation of God in Jesus Christ in the real context of liberation theology? Is biblical speech about God as father and Jesus Christ as son a mirror image of patriarchal social relationships? Does a male savior not come into the consideration of women? Must Christology necessarily be rewritten in order to eliminate any gender differences?

A Note of Encouragement

- First, it may come as a surprise that empirical feminist research assesses the view that women in parishes have of Jesus differently (than professional feminist theologians).[59] The most striking result of one empirical study is the claim that "for no woman does Jesus Christ assume the central role that one would presume in relation to women's consciously Christian religiosity. In this regard, they are different from both traditional as well as liberation-theologically oriented feminist theologies." Jesus of Nazareth does not play a role with regard to the "gender question"; rather, he has a clearly defined meaning for women "as an 'ethical Jesus' and founder of the church community." The conclusion of the empirical study is this: "There is nothing to indicate a direct strengthening of patriarchy." Thus, we see that

59. Following citations from Taube et al., *Frauen und Jesus Christus*, 195, 198.

in the humanistic image of Jesus the lines of feminist theology converge with those of the "congregational theology of women."

- We may simply concede that Christology is useless to liberation theology when, through forcible reinterpretation of the ancient church's Christology, liberation is understood as the revolutionary idea of the social reshaping of the world (such as in the current of neo-Marxist ideas). Redemption is not (as in mythical or Gnostic ideas) the acquiring of a condition that can be planned and enforced in the here and now. It is rather an event that here and now can be experienced in only a fragmentary way and whose completion is still pending. Wherever this eschatological view is lacking, there can ultimately be no hope for the actual *experience of redemption.* Otherwise, there would be simply no waking up from the nightmare of the individually lived history of oppression and injustice, particularly that of women. This redemption transcends gender history and the history of humankind and must be thought of in *cosmic* terms. *The entire creation* will be redeemed, also nature and the animal world—and in the Pauline sense it is about nothing less than the redemption of the universe (Rom 8:22).

- Christology is highly useful to liberation theology when it comes to the interpretation of and perspective on suffering in the world (as was seen in connection with Bonhoeffer's interpretation perspectives for liberation theology in the ocntext context of South Africa). In Jesus Christ, God takes part in the suffering of his creation, but this suffering does not have the last word. Resurrection hope is the basis of the hope of believing Christians in the liberation from suffering, in the overcoming of evil, even of death—it is the great "counter-concept," the hidden other story of God with the world, *his* plan for salvation. It is the tension of Good Friday and Easter, of *kenosis* and the cosmic victory of God's goodness and power. This connection is not obscured by the ancient church's Christology, but illuminated—transcending every gender-specific approach.

- "Classical" Christology does not need to be rewritten (neither by moralizing, mystifying, nor aestheticizing) if its basic tenets are accepted, namely, the positive inexpressibility of the mystery of the person of Jesus Christ, which stands behind the privative alpha of the Chalcedonian Creed. Jesus Christ is always going to be different from any picture of him, be it patriarchal or matriarchal. To cite Susanne Heine: "Jesus Christ and not Jesa Christa. Jesus Christ, the man, who is a stranger even to men."[60]

- The feminist revision of the Christology of the Son represents a break not only with the teaching of the Christian faith, but already with New Testament tradition. Christian language in prayer, liturgy, as well as in theology is bound, for reasons of the theology of revelation, to Jesus' address of God as father and to the Son-Christology associated with it. For "on the lips of Jesus, the appellation of God as 'father' has become a proper name. It has therefore ceased to be one description of God among others."[61] Thus it cannot simply be replaced by a mother-address or a diffuse Sophialogy. Also, biblical speech about God is not simply a mirror image of patriarchal social relationships, but is critical toward them throughout.[62] To superimpose differences in gender on an understanding of God, or to contrast God, whom Jesus called his father, with Sophia, is to reproduce an ultimately heathen view of God.[63] One may say: "In its criticism of biblical monotheism and Son-Christology, radical theological feminism corresponds noticeably to the neopagan character of the 'postmodern' modernity."[64]

---

60. Heine, *Wiederbelebung der Göttinnen?*, 162.
61. Pannenberg, *Systematic Theology*, 1:262.
62. Ibid., 284–86.
63. Cf. Bouyer, *Frau und Kirche*, 54f.
64. Hoping, *Einführung in die Christologie*, 19.

7

Speaking of Christ Today—
Some Room for Encouragement

What should I tell my theology students when they are confronted with the well-meaning or mischievous question, "And what are you studying?" I admit that an ever appropriate answer will not necessarily emerge from the discussions set forth in this volume, certainly not one for those who, for reasons good or not so good, go through life without faith (in God).

But there is another group, not just at student parties: I would like to call it, as does Peter L. Berger,[1] the group of those who are "interested in religion." For them it is clear that religious faith is always based essentially on a basic premise—"that there is a reality beyond the reality of ordinary, everyday life, and that this deeper reality is benign."[2] Perhaps there is one or another person from this group who has had a "transcendent experience" (Berger), which comes up in conversation. And whether or not the experience involved negative or positive signs (or experiences) of transcendence that make someone suddenly see clearly that there is more to reality than one had previously thought: attending to a dying person, the experience of powerlessness and suffering in light of a great injustice, the uncontrollable joy over the birth of the first child, the love for another person. For all of those who express an interest in religion

---

1. Berger, *Questions of Faith*, 1.
2. Ibid.

generally and in Christianity in particular, there are hopefully one or more clues from the previous discussion to support the claim that occupation with the core of the Christian faith can be exciting and important—especially in connection with questions (irrespective of how they arose) we ask about the reasons for joy, the meaning of life, or even the "last things" (Bonhoeffer), but also about the meaning or meaninglessness of suffering.

Admittedly, Christology can be described on the outside only as an arid intellectual skeleton within a larger historical movement (D. Ritschl). But, in the same breath, should we not also admit that it has had an amazingly strong influence? Could this have something to do with what, valid in particular for Christian faith, Peter L. Berger formulates in general terms: "Religion implies that reality ultimately makes sense in human terms. It is the most audacious thought that human beings have ever had. It may be an illusion; even so, it is a very *interesting* one."[3]

Perhaps this excursion into Christology has awakened something of an *interest* in it and made clear why, in view of modern-day challenges, it is worth the trouble to think about Jesus of Nazareth. Such reflections are helpful in that one is not left entirely defenseless in the face of today's objections. Indeed, if it is true that in Jesus Christ something definitive and new has arrived in the life of the individual believer and the whole world, then it is not only worth the effort to think about him, but it is also worth it to challenge the arguments against this position, or—in the words of Foucault—to initiate a counter-discourse.

Thus, there is no good reason to be disconcerted on account of the new and old voices who charge Christian theology with an inability for dialogue and with intolerance. A real plunge into the central questions of how faith comes about at all leads readily and without coercion into a "pluralism of faith." Neither the moralizing insight of the equivalence of the great religions (Lessing), nor the powerful de-absolutizing of the Christian faith (Hick) leads to dialogue, but rather the simple insight that faith in Jesus Christ as savior and redeemer is a gift. The Christian faith does not choose itself or its God, nor does it understand faith as a private matter. The engagement with

3. Ibid.

Christology leads to the insight that trust in God always comes as a result of the revelation of God. Whoever views faith as a gift can indeed be truly tolerant—not only with other religions, but above all with Judaism, which has a special place among all of the religions from the Christian perspective. The God who makes himself known in Jesus of Nazareth is the God of Israel, not a "second God." A good knowledge of Christology (key word: *homoousios*!) can help bring an Israel-affirming Christology into dialogue: Jesus of Nazareth comes from Israel and indeed he is Christ for Christians only because he was the Jew Jesus.

In addition, one need not be insecure when historical research puts the truth-content of the New Testament into question, as in the phrase "when it comes to Jesus, everything is faith." Or: What really happened historically, and how, alone is it true (Ranke)? Such a modern historical concept of truth has fairly well been superseded, or is at the very least naive.[4] Moreover, from the religious side of the argument, the question is on what convictions of faith are based. We only need to consider Buddhists and how little they would make themselves dependent on detailed historical knowledge of their great model. Is it not a testimony of faith that the Bible is very much like a sermon (rather than a historical document)? Does the great gift of faith not become evident precisely in its being testimony from Easter? And does not this great history, which arises from faith in the Easter resurrection, in any case create a deeper certainty than every bit of detailed historical knowledge about Jesus of Nazareth (for example, whether he wore sandals, or preached on the plains, or in the mountains, etc.) would? Furthermore, in my opinion, a certain amount of historical insecurity offers protection against Christian fundamentalism. The idea that there is *one* biblical image of Jesus in the *one* message that we can cull from the New Testament at any time and in any place and can have ownership of has fortunately been uncovered as a construct by political ethics as well as by interreligious dialogue.

On the other hand, there is also no reason to speak disparagingly of the teachings of early Christianity—as in the maxim "the whole thing is cold dogmatism!" Were these dogmas not attempts to

---

4. On the concept of truth in religious-worldly pluralism, see the apt remarks by Schwöbel, *Christlicher Glaube im Pluralismus*, 25–60.

guard the mystery of the person of Christ? Clearly, the occupation with the theme provides a clue to this. Why should it *per se* be bad to occupy one's mind with the divine in Jesus of Nazareth? Should not everyone—whether Christian, atheist, or agnostic—ask themselves on what basis their convictions are built and present them in a thoughtful fashion? Doesn't this belong to the intellectual integrity of every human being? And why do we Protestants have something against dogma? Should we not also promote a Protestant understanding of dogma, whose function it is simply to provide orientation in the tangle of religious convictions—both then as now? Dogmas do not replace what they regulate—namely, the content of the biblical and postbiblical abundance of proclamation and instruction and metaphor. Also, we should not forget that without the "intellectual" arguments about the person of Jesus of Nazareth there would never have been the binding, orienting claim that *God* truly meets us in the *human being* Jesus.

There is also little reason to continue to entertain the idea that the Christian God is a particularly horrible one who takes joy in casting a bloody drama with his son. Occupying oneself with Christology is worthwhile, for then the opposite view comes to light: God does not allow Jesus to suffer, but God himself suffers in that he has bound himself up with human nature in order to reconcile the world with himself. Can one think of something more lofty than a God who takes part in the suffering of his own creation in order to lead it to a greater goal: to its redemption? Here we have a God who does not take guilt lightly—when it comes to redemption, there is no simple "forgive and forget." In that he gives himself up for the sake of reconciliation, all ideas of sacrifice are fulfilled unsurpassably. Thus, Christian soteriology is not regressive but decisively future-oriented: In the death of Jesus Christ any institutionalized cult of sacrifice, be it religious or political, is in the truest sense brought to an end and, in a certain manner, itself "sacrificed."

Finally, all those who occupy themselves intently with christological questions need not be disconcerted by the feminist argument that Christology is of no use to liberation theology. For, in the first place, it is useful after all! At least as long as one understands "liberation" as the attainment of an egalitarian condition of peace within the horizon of history. But because of its utopian-transfigurative nature (be it mystical, aesthetic, or ideological) this assumption masks the historical suffering of people and creatures in the here and now, and takes away the hope of actual redemption. The hope of the resurrection is the basis of hope for believing Christians in liberation from suffering, for the "real" (not ideological, mystical, etc.) overcoming of evil, even of death—that great "counter-concept"—the hidden "other," history of God with the world, his plan for redemption. To offer the consolation that is within the christological horizon is certainly the more realistic and christologically more relevant option vis-à-vis ideological theories for changing the world: the fate of Jesus makes clear that suffering does not have the last word. Good Friday is followed by Easter Sunday! Much is to be said in support of a new political theology in line with Bonhoeffer's ethics, a political theology that neither leaves the sphere of the political to itself, nor coercibly manufactures correspondences between the political and the religious with the help of analogies. Rather, the "signs of the times" require an interpretation that discerns the uniqueness of a "politics of reconciliation" with respect and which—without inserting these signs into a liberation-theologial program or, in Lutheran parlance, turning the gospel into law—may even recognize that Christ is active in the midst of the world.

Jesus Christ is always different from the image we have of him, be it patriarchal or matriarchal. This is exactly what "classical" Christology taught with its rejection of the notion that we can make definitive articulations of Jesus Christ. In his person he remains a mystery. But if it is true that with Jesus Christ something new and decisive has arrived in the life of the individual believer and in the midst of the entire world, then it is not only worth it to reflect on him, but to also accept the challenges and to be encouraged to speak in theological terms about Jesus—particularly today.

Bibliography

Abelard, Peter. *Petri Abaelardi opera*. Edited by Victor Cousin. 2 vols. Paris: A Durand, 1849–59.
Althaus, Paul. *The So-Called Kerygma and the Historical Jesus*. Translated by David Cairns. Edinburgh: Oliver & Boyd, 1959.
Andresen, C., ed. *Handbuch der Dogmen- und Theologiegeschichte*. 3 vols. Göttingen: Vandenhoeck & Ruprecht, 1982.
Anselm of Canterbury. *Cur Deus Homo*. Translated by Sidney Norton Deane. La Salle, IL: Open Court, 1944.
Aulén, Gustaf. *Christus Victor: An Historical Study of the Three Main Types of the Idea of Atonement*. Translated by A. G. Hebert. New York: Macmillan, 1951.
———. "Die drei Haupttypen des christlichen Versöhnungsgedankens." *Zeitschrift für Systematische Theologie* 8 (1930) 501–38.
Barth, Karl. *Church Dogmatics IV/3: The Doctrine of Reconciliation: Jesus Christ, the True Witness*. Edited by G. W. Bromiley and T. F. Torrance. New York: T. & T. Clark, 2009.
———. *Fides quaerens intellectum: Anselms Beweis der Existenz Gottes im Zusammenhang seines theologischen Programms, 1931*. Edited by Eberhard Jüngel and. Ingolf U. Dalferth. 2nd ed. Zürich: Theologischer,1986
———. *Klärung und Wirkung*. Edited by Walter Feurich. Berlin: Union, 1966.
Bartsch, Hans-Werner, ed. *Kerygma and Myth: A Theological Debate*. 2 vols. Translated by Reginald H. Fuller. 2 vols. London: SPCK, 1953–1962.
———, ed. *Kerygma und Mythos: Ein theologisches Gespräch*. 2 vols. Hamburg: Reich, 1952.
Baur, Christian F. *Das Christentum und die christliche Kirche der drei ersten Jahrhunderte*. Tübingen: Allan Menzies, 1853.
Berger, Peter L. *Questions of Faith: A Sceptical Affirmation of Christianity*. Malden, MA: Blackwell, 2004.
Bernhardt, Reinhold, and Ulrike Link-Wieczorek, eds. *Metapher und Wirklichkeit: Die Logik der Bildhaftigkeit im Reden von Gott, Mensch und Natur. Dietrich Ritschl zum 70 Geburtstag*. Göttingen: Vandenhoeck & Ruprecht, 1999.

BIBLIOGRAPHY

Bonhoeffer, Dietrich. *Berlin, 1932–1933*. Edited by Larry L. Rasmussen. Translated by Isabel Best and David Higgins. Dietrich Bonhoeffer Works 12. Minneapolis: Fortress, 2009.

———. *Christology*. Translated by E. Robertson. New York: Harper & Row, 1966.

———. *Discipleship*. Edited by Geffrey D. Kelly and John D. Godsey. Translated by Barbara Green and Reinhard Krauss. Dietrich Bonhoeffer Works 4. Minneapolis: Fortress, 2001.

———. *Ethics*. Edited by Clifford J. Green. Translated by Reinhard Krauss, Charles C. West, and Douglas W. Stott. Dietrich Bonhoeffer Works 6. Minneapolis: Fortress, 2005.

———. *Letters and Papers from Prison*. Edited by Eberhard Bethge. New York: Macmillan, 1972.

———. "Meditation on Christmas, December 1939." In *Theological Education Underground, 1937–40*, edited by Victoria J. Barnett, translated by Victoria J. Barnett et al., 537–43. Dietrich Bonhoeffer Works 15. Minneapolis: Fortress, 2012.

———. *Who Is Christ for Us?* Translated by Craig L. Nessan. Minneapolis: Fortress, 2002.

Bouyer, Louis. *Frau und Kirche*. Einsiedeln: Johannes, 1977.

Braaten, Carl E. *No Other Gospel! Christianity Among the World's Religions*. Minneapolis: Fortress, 1992.

Brunner, Emil. *The Mediator: A Study of the Central Doctrine of the Christian Faith*. Translated by Olive Wyon. Philadelphia: Westminster, 1947.

Bultmann, Rudolf. "Das christologische Bekenntnis des Ökumenischen Rates." In *Glauben und Verstehen: Gessamelte Aufsätze*, 4 vols., 2:246–61. Tübingen: Mohr (Siebeck), 1952.

Essays, Philosophical and Theological. Translated by James C. G. Greig. New York: Macmillan, 1955.

———. *Faith and Understanding*. Translated by Louise Pettibone Smith. New York: Harper & Row, 1969.

———. *The New Testament and Mythology and Other Basic Writings*. Selected, edited, and translated by Schubert M. Ogden. Philadelphia: Fortress, 1984.

———. *Theology of the New Testament*. Translated by Kendrick Grobel. 2 vols. New York: Scribner's, 1951–1955.

Calvin, John. *Institutes of the Christian Religion*. Edited by John T. McNeill. Translated by Ford Lewis Battles. Philadelphia: Westminster, 1960.

Conway, E. *The Anonymous Christian—a Relativised Christianity? An Evaluation of Hans Urs von Balthasar's Criticisms of Karl Rahner's Theory of the Aonymous Christian*. Frankfurt am Main: P. Lang, 1993.

Dalferth, Ingolf U. *Der auferweckte Gekreuzigte. Zur Grammatik der Christologie*. Tübingen: Mohr Siebeck, 1994.

———. "Volles Grab, leerer Glaube? Zum Streit um die Auferweckung des Gekreuzigten." *Zeitschrift für Theologie und Kirche* 95 (1998) 379–409.

BIBLIOGRAPHY

Dalferth, Ingolf U., and Hans-Peter Grosshans, eds. *Kritik der Religion: Zur Aktualität einer underledigten philosophischen und theologischen Aufgabe.* Tübingen: Mohr Siebeck, 2006.

Daly, Mary. *Beyond God the Father: Toward a Philosophy of Women's Liberation.* Boston: Beacon, 1973.

Daub, Hans Friedrich. *Die Stellvertretung Jesu Christi. Ein Aspekt des Gott-Mensch-Verhältnisses bei Dietrich Bonhoeffer.* Berlin: Lit, 2006.

De Gruchy, John W. "Christian Witness in a Secular State." In *An African Challenge to the Church in the 21st Century*, edited by Mongezi Guma and Leslie Milton, 86–96. Johannesburg: SACC, 1997.

Dembowski, Hermann. *Einführung in die Christologie.* Darmstadt: Wissenschaftliche Buchgesellschaft, 1976.

Elert, Werner. *Morphologie des Luthertums.* Vol. 1. Munich: Beck, 1931.

Fischer, Hans Rudi, ed. *Die Wirklichkeit des Konstruktivismus: Zur Auseinandersetzung um ein neues Paradigma.* Heidelberg: Carl-Auer-Systeme, 1995.

Forst, Rainer, ed. *Toleranz: Philosophische Grundlagen und gesellschaftliche Praxis einer umstrittenen Tugend.* Frankfurt: Campus, 2000.

Gäde, Gerhard. *Eine andere Barmherzigkeit. Zum Verständnis der Erlösungslehre Anselms von Canterbury.* Bonner Dogmatische Schriften 3. Würzburg: Echter, 1989.

Gerber, Uwe. *Christologische Entwürfe. Ein Arbeitsbuch. I Von der Reformation bis zur Dialektischen Theologie.* Zürich: EVZ, 1970.

Gogarten, Friedrich. *Christ the Crisis.* Translated by R. A. Wilson. Richmond: John Knox, 1970.

Goldenberg, Naomi. *Changing of the Gods: Feminism and the End of Traditional Religions.* Boston: Beacon, 1979.

Göttner-Abendroth, Heide. *Die transzendente Göttin: Prinzipien einer matriarchalen Ästhetik.* Munich: Frauenoffensive, 1984.

Günther, Ernst. *Die Entwicklung der Lehre von der Person Christi im XIX. Jahrhundert.* Tübingen: J. C. B. Mohr, 1911.

Halkes, Catharina. *Suchen, was verlorenging: Beiträge zur feministischen Theologie.* Gütersloh: Gerd Mohn, 1985.

Härle, Wilfried. "Aus dem Heiligen Geist. Positioneller Pluralismus als christliche Konsequenz." *Die Zeichen der Zeit* 37 (1998) 21–24.

———. *Dogmatik.* 2nd ed. Berlin: de Gruyter, 2000.

———. "Gott fürchten und liebe. Martin Luther und die Kunst lebenswichtiger Unterscheidungen." In *Nimm und lies! Theologische Quereinstiege für Neugierige*, edited by Ralf K. Wüstenberg, 110–25. Gütersloh: Gerd Mohn, 2008.

Harnack, Adolf von. *What Is Christianity?* Translated by Thomas Bailey Saunders. Philadelphia: Fortress, 1986, 1957.

Heim, Karl. "Die Haupttypen der Versöhnungslehre." *Zeitschrift für Theologie und Kirche* 19 (1938) 304–19.

BIBLIOGRAPHY

Heine, Susanne. *Wiederbelebung der Göttinnen? Zur systematischen Kritik einer feministischen Theologie.* Göttingen: Vandenhoeck & Ruprecht, 1987.

Herms, E. "Pluralismus aus Prinzip." In *"Vor Ort": Praktische Theologie in der Erprobung. Festschrift zum 60. Geburtstag von Peter C. Bloth,* edited by Rainer Bookhagen et al., 95-124. Nuremberg: Stoja, 1991.

Herrmann, Wilhelm. *The Communion of the Christian with God on the Basis of Luther's Statements.* Translated by J. Sandys Stanyon. New York: Putnam, 1913.

Heyward, Carter. *Und sie rührte sein Kleid an: Eine feministische Theologie der Beziehung.* Stuttgart: Kreuz, 1989.

Hick, John. *An Interpretation of Religion: Human Response to the Transcendent.* New Haven: Yale University Press, 1989.

―――. *The Myth of God Incarnate.* Philadelphia: Westminster, 1977.

Hoping, Helmut. *Einführung in die Christologie.* Darmstadt: Wissenschaftliche Buchgesellschaft, 2004.

Hopkins, Julie. *Towards a Feminist Christology.* Grand Rapids: Eerdmans, 1994.

Huber, Wolfgang. *Kirche und Öffentlichkeit.* Forschungen und Berichte der Evangelischen Studiengemeinschaft 28. Stuttgart: Klett, 1973.

―――, ed. *Schuld und Versöhnung in politischer Perspektive: Dietrich-Bonhoeffer-Vorlesungen in Berlin.* Internationales Bonhoeffer Forum, Forshung und Praxis 10. Gütersloh: Kaiser, 1996.

Jüngel, Eberhard. *God as the Mystery of the World: On the Foundation of the Theology of the Crucified One in the Dispute between Theism and Atheism.* Translated by Darrell L. Guder. Grand Rapids: Eerdmans, 1983.

Kähler, Martin. *The So-Called Historical Jesus and the Historical Biblical Christ.* Translated by Carl Braaten. Philadelphia: Fortress, 1988.

Kampling, Rainer, and Michael Weinrich. *Dabru emet—redet Wahrheit. Eine jüdische Herausforderung zum Dialog mit den Christen.* Gütersloh: Kaiser, 2003.

Karpp, Heinrich, ed. *Textbuch zur altkirchlichen Christologie. Theologia und Oikonomia.* Neukirchen-Vluyn: Neukirchener, 1972.

Käsemann, Ernst. "The Problem of the Historical Jesus." In *Essays on New Testament Themes,* translated by W. J. Montague, 15-47. London: SCM, 1964.

Kettler, F. H. "Versöhnung, dogmengeschichtlich." In *Religion in Geschichte und Gegenwart,* edited by Hans Dieter Betz et al., 6:1373-78. Tübingen: Mohr Siebeck, 1998-2005.

Kirn, O. "Versöhnung." *Realencyklopädie für protestantische Theologie und Kirche* 20 (1908) 552-76.

Klappert, Bertold. *Versöhnung und Befreiung. Versuche, Karl Barth kontextuell zu verstehen* Neukirchener Beiträge zur systematischen Theologie 14. Neukirchen-Vluyn: Neukirchener, 1994.

Klinger, Elmar. *Christologie im Feminismus: Eine Herausforderung der Tradition.* Regensburg: Pustet, 2001.

BIBLIOGRAPHY

Knitter, Paul F. *One Earth, Many Religions: Multifaith Dialogue and Global Responsibility*. Maryknoll, NY: Orbis, 1995.

Kühn, Ulrich. *Christologie*. Uni-Taschenbücher 2393. Stuttgart: Vandenhoeck & Ruprecht, 2003.

Küng, Hans. *Global Responsibility: In Search of a New World Ethic*. 1991. Reprint, Eugene, OR: Wipf & Stock, 2004.

Kuschel, Karl-Josef. *Jesus im Spiegel der Weltliteratur: Eine Jahrhundertbilanz in Texten und Einführungen*. Düsseldorf: Patmos, 1999.

———. *Jud, Christ und Muselmann vereinigt: Lessings "Nathan, der Weise"*. Düsseldorf: Patmos, 2004.

———. *Juden, Christen, Muslime: Herkunft und Zukunft*. Düsseldorf: Patmos, 2007.

Lange, Dietz. *Historischer Jesus oder mythischer Christus. Untersuchungen zum Gegensatz zwischen F. Schleiermacher und D. F. Strauß*. Gütersloh: Gerd Mohn, 1975.

Lapide, Pinchas, and Karl Rahner. *Heil von den Juden: Ein Gespräch*. Mainz: Matthias Grünewald, 1983.

Lehmkühler, Karsten. "Christologie." In *Bonhoeffer und Luther: Zentrale Themen ihrer Theologie*, edited by Klaus Grünwald et al., 55–78. Hannover: Amt der VELKD, 2007.

Luther, Martin. *Against Latomus*. Translated by George Lindbeck. In *Career of the Reformer II*, edited by George W. Forell, 133–260. Luther's Works 32. Philadelphia: Muhlenberg, 1958.

———. "Confession Concerning Christ's Supper." In *Martin Luther's Basic Theological Writings*, edited by Timothy Lull, 50–62. Minneapolis: Fortress, 1989.

———. "The Freedom of a Christian." In *Martin Luther's Basic Theological Writings*, edited by Timothy Lull, 585–629. Minneapolis: Fortress, 1989.

———. *The Freedom of a Christian*. Translated by Mark Tranvik. Minneapolis: Fortress, 2008.

Marquardt, Friedrich-Wilhelm. "The Christian Confession of Jesus the Jew." In *Jews and Christians: Rivals or Partners for the Kingdom of God? In Search of an Alternative for the Theology of Substitution*, edited by Didier Pollefeyt, 50–51. Louvain: Peeters, 1997.

———. *Das christliche Bekenntnis zu Jesus, dem Juden : eine Christologie*. 2 vols. Munich: Kaiser, 1990–1991.

Marquardt, Odo von. *Abschied vom Prinzipiellen: Philosophische Studien*. Stuttgart: Reclam, 1986.

Menke, Karl-Heinz. *Die Einzigkeit Jesu Christi im Horizont der Sinnfrage*. Freiburg: Johannes, 1995.

Moltmann, Jürgen. *Jesus Christ for Today's World*. Translated by Margaret Kohl. Minneapolis: Fortress, 1994.

———. *The Way of Jesus Christ: Christology in Messianic Dimensions*. Translated by Margaret Kohl. San Francisco: Harper & Row, 1990.

---. *Der Weg Jesu Christi: Christologie in messianischen Dimensionen.* Munich: Chr-Kaiser, 1989

Moltmann-Wendel, Elisabeth. "Gibt es eine feministische Rechtfertigungslehre?" *Evangelische Theologie* 60 (2000) 348–59.

Moser, S. *Komplexe Konstruktionen: Systemtheorie, Konstruktivismus und Literaturwissenschaft.* Wiesbaden: Deutscher Universitäts-Verlag, 2001.

Mulack, Christa. *Die Weiblichkeit Gottes: Matriarchale Voraussetzungen des Gottesbildes.* Stuttgart: Kreuz, 1983.

Ott, Heinrich. "Anselms Versöhnungslehre." *Theologische Zeitschrift* 13 (1957) 183–338.

Pannenberg, Wolfhart. *Grundzüge der Christologie.* Göttingen: Vandenhoeck & Ruprecht, 1976.

---. *Systematic Theology.* Translated by Geoffrey W. Bromiley. 3 vols. Grand Rapids: Eerdmans, 1991–98.

Plant, Stephen. *Bonhoeffer.* Outstanding Christian Thinkers. New York: Continuum, 2004.

Plasger, Georg. *Die Not-Wendigkeit der Gerechtigkeit. Eine Interpretation zu "Cur Deus Homo" von Anselm von Canterbury.* Beiträge zur Geschichte der Philosophie und Theologie des Mittelalters., N. F., 38. Münster: Aschendorff, 1993.

Plaskow, Judith. *Sex, Sin, and Grace: Women's Experience and the Theologies of Reinhold Niebuhr and Paul Tillich.* Washington, DC: University Press of America, 1980.

Rad, Gerhard von. *Theologie des Alten Testaments.* 2 vols. 4th ed. Munich: 1965–66.

Ratschow, Carl Heinz. *Jesus Christus.* Gütersloh: Gerd Mohn, 1982.

Rendtorff, Trutz. "Die Zweireichelehre oder die Kunst des Unterscheidens, Bemerkungen zur theologischen Deutung des Politischen." In *Zwei Reiche und Regimente: Ideologie oder evangelische Orientierung?*, edited by Ulrich Duchrow. Gütersloh: Gerd Mohn, 1977.

Ritschl, Albrecht. *The Christian Doctrine of Justification and Reconciliation.*

---. *Die christliche Lehre von der Rechtfertigung und Versöhnung.* Vol. 1. 4th ed. Bonn: Adolph Marcus, 1885.

Ritschl, Dietrich. "Gotteserkenntnis durch Wiederkennen." In *Einfach von Gott reden: ein theologischer Diskurs. Festschrift für Friedrich Mildenberger zum 65. Geburtstag*, edited by Jürgen Roloff and Hans G. Ulrich, 144–52. Stuttgart: Kohlhammer, 1994.

Ritschl, Dietrich, and Martin Hailer. *Diesseits und jenseits der Worte: Grundkurs christliche Theologie.* Neukirchen-Vluyn: Neukirchener, 2006.

Rogge, Joachim, and Helmut Zeddies. *Kirchengemeinschaft und politische Ethik: Ergebnis eines theologischen Gesprächs zum Verhältnis von Zwei-reiche-Lehre und Lehre von der Königsherrschaft Christi.* Berlin: Evangelische, 1980.

Rosenau, Hartmut. "Möglichkeiten und Grenzen einer theologischen Begründung der Toleranz." In *Religionsunterricht interreligiös:*

BIBLIOGRAPHY

hermeneutische und didaktische Erschliessungen: Festschrift für Folkert Rickers zum 65. Geburtstag, edited by Eckart Gottwald and Norbert Mette, 218–26. Neukirchen: Neukirchen-Vluyn, 2003.

Ruether, Rosemary Radford. *Faith and Fratricide: The Theological Roots of Anti-Semitism*. New York: Seabury, 1974.

———. *Nächstenliebe und Brudermord: Die theologischen Wurzeln des Antisemitismus*. Munich: Kaiser, 1978

———. *Sexism and God-Talk: Toward a Feminist Theology*. Boston: Beacon, 1983.

Rumscheidt, Martin. *Revelation and Theology: An Analysis of the Barth-Harnack Corresponence of 1923*. 1972. Reprint, Eugene, OR: Wipf and Stock, 2011.

Sauter, Gerhard, ed. *"Versöhnung" als Thema der Theologie*. Theologische Bücherei 92. Gütersloh: Kaiser, 1997.

Scherzberg, Lucia. *Sünde und Gnade in der feministischen Theologie*. Mainz: Matthias Grünewald, 1991.

Schilling, Johannes. *Martin Luther, Lateinisch-deutsche Studienausgabe*. Vol. 2, *Christusglaube und Rechtfertigung*. Leipzig: Evangelische Verlagsanstalt, 2006.

Schleiermacher, Friedrich D. E. *The Christian Faith*. Edited by H. R. Mackintosh and J. S. Stewart. 2 vols. New York: Harper & Row, 1963.

Schmidt-Leukel, Perry. "Das pluralistische Modell in der Theologie der Religionen. Ein Literaturbericht." *Theologische Revue* 89 (1993) 353–64.

Schüssler Fiorenza, Elisabeth. *In Memory of Her: A Feminist Theological Reconstruction of Christian Origins*. New York: Crossroad, 1983.

Schwöbel, Christoph. *Christlicher Glaube im Pluralismus*. Tübingen: Mohr Siebeck, 2003.

Seiger, Bernhard. *Versöhnung, Gabe und Aufgabe. Eine Untersuchung zur neueren Bedeutungsentwicklung eines theologischen Begriffs*. Europäische Hochschulschriften, Series 23, Theology 563. Frankfurt am Main: P. Lang, 1996.

Shriver, Donald W. *An Ethic for Enemies. Forgiveness in Politics*. New York: Oxford University Press, 1995.

Simonis, Walter. *Jesus Christus, wahrer Mensch und unser Herr*. Düsseldorf: Patmos, 2004.

Simos, Miriam. *Die Kraft der großen Göttin*. Freiburg: Bauer, 1999.

Sölle, Dorothee. *Lieben und Arbeiten: Eine Theologie der Schöpfung*. Stuttgart: Kreuz, 1986.

Sorge, Elga. *Religion und Frau: Weibliche Spiritualität im Christentum*. 2nd ed. Stuttgart: Kohlhammer, 1987.

Stauffer, Ethelbert. *Jesus war ganz anders*. Hamburg: Wittig, 1967.

Steiger, Johann Anselm. "Aufklärungskritische Versöhnungslehre. Zorn Gottes, Opfer Christi und Versöhnung in der Theologie Justus Christoph Krafcts, Friedrich Gottlieb Klopstocks und Christian Friedrich Daniel Schubarts." *Pietismus und Neuzeit* 20 (1994) 125–72.

———. "Die communicatio idiomatum als Achse und Motor der Theologie Luthers. Der 'fröhliche Wechsel' als hermeneutischer Schlüssel zu Abendmahlslehre, Anthropologie, Seelsorge, Naturlehre, Rhetorik und Humor." *Neue Zeitschrift für Systematische Theologie* 38 (1996) 1–28.

Strahm, Doris, et al., eds. *Vom Verlangen nach Heilwerden: Christologie in feministisch-theologischer Sicht*. Freiburg: Luzern, 1993.

Strobel, Regula. "Feministisch-theologische Kritik an Kreuzestheologien." *Katechetische Blätter* 2 (1998) 84–90.

Sundermeier, Theo. "Erlösung oder Versöhnung." *Evangelische Theologie* 53 (1993) 124–46.

Szenpétery, Peter. "Ist die 'Nachfolge' eine radikale Kritik der Luthertums?" In *Bonhoeffer und Luther: Zentrale Themen ihrer Theologie*, edited by Klaus Grünwald et al., 144–66. Hannover: Amt der VELKD, 2007.

Taube, Roselies, et al. *Frauen und Jesus Christus: Die Bedeutung von Christologie im Leben protestantischer Frauen*. Stuttgart: Kohlhammer, 1995.

Theissen, Gerd. *Verhalten und Erleben der ersten Christen: Eine Psychologies des Urchristentums*. Gütersloh: Gerd Mohn, 2007.

Thomasius, Gottfried. *Beiträge zur kirchlichen Christologie*. Erlangen: Theodor Bläsing, 1845.

Tillich, Paul. *Systematic Theology*. 3 vols. Chicago: University of Chicago Press, 1951–1963.

Troeltsch, Ernst. *The Absoluteness of Christianity and the History of Religions*. Translated by David Reid. Louisville: Westminster John Knox, 2005.

———. *Die Absolutheit des Christentums und die Religionsgeschichte* (1902/1912). Berlin/New York: Rendtorff, 1998.

———. *The Social Teaching of the Christian Churches*. 2 vols. Translated by Olive Wyon. Louisville: Westminster John Knox, 1992.

Van Buren, Paul M. *A Theology of the Jewish-Christian Reality, Part 3: Christ in Context*. San Franciso: HarperSanFrancisco, 1988.

Watzlawick, Paul. *Wie wirklich ist die Wirklichkeit? Wahn, Täuschung, Verstehen*. Munich: Piper, 1977.

Welker, Michael. "Elend und Auftrag der nach Gottes Wort reformierten Theologie am Anfang des dritten Jahrtausends." *Reformierte Kirchenzeitung* 140 (1999) 27–36.

———. "Die evangelische Freiheit." *Evangelische Theologie* 57 (1997) 68–73.

———. "Das Reich Gottes." *Evangelische Theologie* 52 (1992) 497–512.

Wenz, Gunther. *Geschichte der Versöhnungslehre in der Evangelischen Theologie der Neuzeit*. 2 vols. Munich: Kaiser, 1984.

Wierlacher, Alois, ed. *Kulturthema Toleranz: Zur Grundlegung einer interdisziplinären Toleranzforschung*. Kulturthemen 2. Munich: Iudicium, 1996.

Willis, David, and Michael Welker, eds. *Toward the Future of Reformed Theology: Tasks, Topics, Traditions*. Grand Rapids: Eerdmans, 1999.

Wirsching, Johannes. "Gottes Heilstat und menschliche Freiheit: Grundmotive in der Inkarnationslehre Anselms von Canterbury." In *Glaube im*

Widerstreit: Ausgewählte Aufsätze und Vorträge, 2:75-84. Frankfurt am Main: P. Lang, 1993.

———. "Menschwerdung: Von der wahren Gestalt des Göttlichen." In *Die Weltlichkeit des Glaubens in der Alten Kirche: Festschrift für Ulrich Wickert zum siebzigsten Geburtstag*, edited by Dietmar Wyrwa with Barbara Aland and Christoph Schäublin, 399-441. New York: de Gruyter, 1997.

Wüstenberg, Ralf K. "Bonhoeffer 'Revisited': Religionslosigkeit und nichtreligiöse Interpretation im 21. Jahrhundert." *Theologische Literaturzeitung* 131 (2006) 129-40.

———. "Der Einwand des Offenbarungspositivismus: Was hat Bonhoeffer eigentlich an Barth kirtisert?" *Theologische Literaturzeitung* 121 (1996) 997-1004.

———. "Fides implicita 'Revisited'—Versuch eines evangelischen Zugangs." *Neue Zeitschrift für Systematische Theologie Und Religionsphilosophie* 49 (2007) 71-85.

———, ed. *Nimm und lies! Theologische Quereinstige für Neugierige*. Gütersloh: Gütersloher Verlagshaus, 2008.

———. *The Political Dimension of Reconciliation: A Theological Analysis of Ways of Dealing with Guilt during the Transition to Democracy in South Africa and (East) Germany*. Translated by Randi Lundell. Grand Rapids: Eerdmans, 2009.

www.ingramcontent.com/pod-product-compliance
Lightning Source LLC
Chambersburg PA
CBHW020855160426
43192CB00007B/932